CURSE OF THE PHARAOHS' TOMBS

For my wonderful grandchildren
Mia, Tom and Abbie

CURSE OF THE PHARAOH'S TOMBS

Tales of the Unexpected
Since the Days of Tutankhamun

Paul Harrison

First published in Great Britain in 2017 by
PEN & SWORD ARCHAEOLOGY
an imprint of
Pen and Sword Books Ltd
47 Church Street
Barnsley
South Yorkshire S70 2AS

ISBN 978 1 78159 366 0

A CIP record for this book is available from the British Library

Printed and bound in England
by CPI Group (UK) Ltd, Croydon, CR0 4YY

Typeset in Times New Roman by
CHIC GRAPHICS

Pen & Sword Books Ltd incorporates the imprints of
Pen & Sword Archaeology, Atlas, Aviation, Battleground, Discovery,
Family History, History, Maritime, Military, Naval, Politics, Railways,
Select, Social History, Transport, True Crime, Claymore Press,
Frontline Books, Leo Cooper, Praetorian Press, Remember When,
Seaforth Publishing and Wharncliffe.

For a complete list of Pen and Sword titles please contact
Pen and Sword Books Limited
47 Church Street, Barnsley, South Yorkshire, S70 2AS, England
E-mail: enquiries@pen-and-sword.co.uk
Website: www.pen-and-sword.co.uk

Contents

Preface

I have studied and researched the subject of ancient Egyptian curses for some time, so it would be fair to say that I possess a plethora of knowledge on the subject. Tales of mysterious goings-on litter historical and modern-day revelations from the land of Egypt. Curses are synonymous with Egypt and, more specifically, with the great pharaohs: stories, myths and legends that have been embellished by countless retellings of a more sinister nature. The curse had an altogether different meaning for the ancient Egyptians than it does today Western culture, which has sensationalised it. For the ancient Egyptians, who embraced death, a curse was a way to maintain law and order and allow the dead pharaoh's soul to successfully traverse through to the afterworld, where they could be reunited with their worldly form and live in Aalu (paradise) for eternity.

I could never have completed this book without the assistance of many other people, too many to list and detail here. Primarily, I want to thank my own family and their continuing belief in my work. The staff of the Cairo museum supported the concept and helped direct me to many sources. The staff of the British museum, who maintained an air of sensibility and level-headedness about the subject, were most helpful in their observations. I wish to thank the team at Pen & Sword for their support and understanding in allowing me time to complete the manuscript, in particular my editors, Eloise Hansen and Heather Williams. My study of ancient Egypt has led me to appreciate the wonder and interest of this era in human history, and I wholeheartedly recommend that readers visit the Great Pyramids, the Sphinx, Cairo, Luxor or the Valley of the Kings (and Queens) if they can.

Introduction

The first legends of the 'curse of the pharaohs' arose sometime in the seventh century, when the first Arabs arrived in Egypt. Unable to read hieroglyphics, they were seemingly confused by what they saw: almost everything in the land was strange and had an air of the mysterious about it. The highly decorated tombs and the incredible mummy preservation ignited all kinds of fantasy in their imaginations, and subsequent stories were based on those initial finds. The Arabs were of the opinion that if they entered a tomb and were able to recite a magical spell, then beautiful rich objects that had been made invisible by the ancient Egyptians would appear before them and be theirs to take. There was also an element of fear, as it was widely believed that the mummies would spring to life again. The Arabs believed the tombs to be protected by magic and curses.

My own fascination with Egyptology began when I was just twelve years old, with a tale that held me spellbound throughout my school life and has continued to captivate me to this day. In 1972, England was gripped by the strange myths and legends and history surrounding a dead Egyptian pharaoh, the boy king, Tutankhamun. A unique exhibition entitled 'Treasures of Tutankhamun' was formally opened at the British Museum, London, on 30 March 1972 by Queen Elizabeth II. The exhibition, which displayed countless priceless artifacts recovered from Tutankhamun's tomb in the Valley of the Kings, was scheduled to run for six months but was so popular that it was extended until the end of December. A total of 1,694,117 visitors (over 7,000 per day) queued to see the objects and curiosities that were on display. The author (then a boy) was one of those fortunate enough to see the wonders discovered by Howard Carter half a century earlier. The exhibition secured my lifetime interest in ancient Egypt and, in particular, because of the beauty of the objects left within the dead pharaoh's tomb, the ancient Egyptians' fascination with death. I keenly read all the literature that was then available on the subject and immersed myself in history. From the outset it was clear that despite our modern civilization we knew relatively little about the ancient Egyptians. This element of the 'unknown' compelled me to learn more. I begin this book, which collects the stories of the curses of the pharoahs' tombs, by recounting a story as it was told to me as a young impressionable child.

It was on Monday 25 November 1922, in Egypt's Valley of the Kings, that archaeologists first unearthed an ancient burial tomb that had been lost for over 3,000 years. This tomb was special for it was the final resting place of the boy pharaoh, Tutankhamun. Carefully the entrance to the tomb was uncovered and the desert sands began to reveal the contents of what has been described as the greatest archaeological find of all time. Gradually, day by day, the contents of the tomb were removed, and it was during this process that strange, unaccountable incidents began to occur. The arduous task of carrying and lifting heavy objects from the tomb fell on the local Arab work force. It came as no surprise when a number fell ill – probably from exhaustion considering the cramped, hot and dusty working conditions – but it is claimed that a number of these people became violently ill, and died during the process of emptying the tomb. A short time later, it was said that two cooks who worked on the excavations were found dead, both drowned in the Nile. More incidents followed, the most high profile of which occurred in March 1923 when Lord Carnarvon, who was the financial benefactor behind the excavations, was allegedly bitten by a mosquito and, as a result of the illness he contracted from the poisoned septic bite, died in Cairo on 5 April 1923. A few weeks later, a nurse who had been treating Carnarvon supposedly said: 'This is a cover up, they know the truth, the death came from the curse of the dead pharaoh, the officials are too frightened to admit it! Carnarvon told me he could see the god of the afterlife (Osiris) awaiting him and the great black jackal (Anubis) watching and waiting. He was frightened, delirious, yet he spoke of seeing these things with great lucidity.' Within days, the press, which had been prevented from covering the precise details of the excavation because *The Times* had previously bought the rights to sole and bespoke coverage, had seized on this new angle on the sensational find in Egypt. Across the world news stories about the excavation of King Tutankhamun's tomb and the so-called curse that was said to have been found in the tomb proved of immense interest to readers, to the delight of the newspaper owners who saw an increase in sales.

However, this story takes us several thousand miles from the Valley of the Kings, to Birmingham in England. Here, in 1970, it is said that the curse of Tutankhamun revealed itself. An antique collector, whose name is unknown but who has been referred to as Mark Wright or John Scott in retellings of the story, was in the city searching for items of rare jewellery that he could sell on at his London-based business. Always looking for a bargain, he visited the various markets and pawn and antique shops across Birmingham. During a trip to a market in St Martin's Circus, he came across some 'different' pieces; they were clearly Egyptian and antique. What interested the buyer most was a brooch that took the form of a scarab beetle. Instinctively he knew it had considerable value and, after a bit of bartering, he bought the brooch for of £67. He put the scarab brooch into his coat pocket and began to make his way back to his hotel in Suffolk Street. During the walk he was surprised to be accosted by an old Egyptian man, who demanded the scarab brooch, saying 'It must be returned to the sand or it will take your life'. This was Idris Fahoud, who claimed to have been at the tomb of King Tutankhamun when the King's sarcophagus had been opened. Fahoud, like many Egyptians, was greatly upset that foreigners were seemingly permitted to plunder the graves of his country's ancient kings and profit from the sale of these valuable historical objects. The new owner of the scarab brooch continued towards his hotel, but Fahoud followed, still pleading with him to give the scarab up.

Once inside the sanctuary of his hotel, the antique collector, who was due back in London the next day, settled his bill and packed his suitcases for an early start. But at 3.11am a blood-curdling scream was heard in the corridors of the second floor of the hotel. Guests came out of their rooms to see what was the matter; the screaming seemed to be coming from room 222. Banging on the locked door brought no response from within. Eventually, a night porter arrived with a pass key, and opened the door. Before him was a gruesome sight. The resident of the room sat upright in the bed, his face contorted in agonising pain, his eyes wide open, staring straight ahead. Blood slowly dripped from his nose. His mouth was wide open but he made no noise: it was as if he was screaming silently. The porter approached, but jumped back as a huge insect, described as the size of large human fist, clambered out of the unfortunate man's mouth. Believing it to be dangerous, the porter moved to catch and stamp on the insect, which dropped to the floor and remained stationary. As the porter neared it, the insect vanished and was never found. An onlooker thought he saw it on top of the dead man's suitcase, but this was the scarab brooch. The porter instructed another guest to call the police and an ambulance, and closed the room door on the other assembled guests, leaving him alone in the room with the body. Unobserved, he put the scarab brooch in his pocket.

When the police eventually arrived at the hotel, Idris Fahoud made himself known to the officers and told them that the man had in his possession a sacred scarab brooch, which was the property of the people of Egypt. Room 222 was thoroughly searched, as were the dead man's possessions, but no scarab brooch was found. Idris Fahoud refused to believe that it could disappear, and accused the night porter of taking it. The police wouldn't listen and told Fahoud to leave. Fahoud lay in wait until he saw the porter alone and confronted him. He called him a thief and a liar, then told him he could expect dire consequences for his theft of the scarab brooch. Two days later, the night porter was admitted to a Birmingham Accident and Emergency Unit, having swallowed a quantity of glass that was in some jam. The man's insides were lacerated and infection had set in. He was close to death. Fahoud managed to get into the hospital to speak to him. He told the porter that he was cursed and that anyone who took or kept the brooch would be cursed too. Now, before the porter died, was the only chance to end the curse by giving the scarab brooch back to its rightful owners. The dying man told Fahoud that the brooch was gone and he did not know where. He had passed it to his daughter and instructed her to return to the market to sell it for whatever she could get for it. She had done so and it had been purchased by a dealer based in Yorkshire. The night porter died a painful death.

Eight years later, in 1978, Idris Fahoud ended his English search for Egyptian antiquities and returned to his homeland with a variety of objects which he claimed belonged to King Tutankhamun. There, he privately took them out to the Valley of the Kings and returned them to the gods and the earth. The events were later retold by Fahoud on his deathbed in a confession to a Cairo newspaper:

'I swear that the curse will remain as long as the body of the boy king remains above the sands of Egypt. Each and every article stolen from the holy shrine of the son of God will bring death to any person who takes possession of it. My work is complete, Osiris awaits, I must go, I go to join my Lord, my task is done.'

Once I heard this story my own fate was sealed: I was hooked and wanted to learn more, not only from books but also through my own research in Egypt and beyond. I went in search of the truth and found myself embracing not only the myths and the legends, but the life the ancient Egyptians enjoyed, and death and the afterlife that followed. In December 2008, while in discussion with some local guides and academic Egyptologists on a journey down the River Nile, I was told of the existence of countless previously unrecorded incidents that have maintained real credibility with many local Egyptian scholars over the years. One man described these tomes as 'the forgotten' or 'the hidden' details, the 'unnatural' as opposed to the 'supernatural'. I wanted to know more and so obtained as much detail from my Egyptian contacts as I was able. The results of the research were fascinating and form the basis of this book, although I suspect a further volume, with a more supernatural and sinister undertone, may follow. Of one thing I am certain: my quest for the truth will never be over. The curse of the pharaohs' tombs will forever intrigue and send shivers down the spine. The ancient Egyptians were intelligent; they created and built many things that continue to defy modern-day understanding. I believe they were more advanced in many matters than we ever will be. Their world was based on belief, brought about through communication and understanding. Today, most civilisations believe in some kind of life after death, just as the ancient Egyptians did. Whether it really exists or not is a matter of opinion or religion; I do not attempt to persuade or dissuade anyone from their own belief. Whatever the truth, ancient

Egyptians did all they could to provide for the soul's well-being after death. Jewellery and other worldly riches were buried with the corpse, which itself was wrapped and mummified it so it too could be of use after death. To protect the valuable grave goods the ancient Egyptians called upon their gods and other supernatural creatures to defend tombs and their contents at all costs, to deter tomb robbers or other act of sacrilege. Thus the legends of the curse of the pharaoh's tomb began.

Paul Harrison
January, 2017

Glossary

Aah – Aah was an ancient moon god of Egypt.

Abdu Heba – Ruler of Jerusalem and a contemporary of Akhenaten.

Abtu-fish – A mythological fish which accompanies the Boat of Ra.

Achenaten, Akhenaten, Akhenaton, Akhnaten, Akhenaton Amenhotep IV – a New Kingdom pharaoh, 18th dynasty.

Ahmose, Amasis 1) Two pharaohs – Ahmose I, 18th dynasty and Ahmose II, 26th dynasty; 2) Ahmose-Nefertiti, Queen of the 18th Dynasty; 3) Ahmose Son of Ebana, admiral under king Ahmose I; 4) Ahmose Pen-nekhbet, high official under Ahmose I.

Aker – Aker was an ancient Egyptian earth god and the deification of the horizon.

Akhet, Shait – Season of inundation, from mid-July to mid-November in Ptolemaic times.

Akhetaten, Al Amarna, El Amarna – Capital of Akhenaten, 18th dynasty.

Akh – Occasionally translated as 'soul'; the state in which the deceased exists in the afterlife, both immortal and unchangeable.

Akhu, akhet – The blessed dead, ancestors.

Amemt – The mythical animal which devours the hearts of the wicked at the Judgment of Osiris.

Amen, Ammon, Amon, Amun, Amoun, Amun-Re or Amen-Re – The main god during the New Kingdom, identified with Zeus by the Greeks.

Menemhab, Amenemheb Amenemhet, Amenemhat – Four pharaohs of the 12th dynasty.

Amenemope, Amenemopet – 1) Family of high New Kingdom officials; 2) Viceroy of Kush under Seti I; 3) Vizier under Amenhotep II

Amenirdis – Wife of the god (high priestess of Amen)

Amenmes – New Kingdom pharaoh, 19th dynasty.

Amenmose – 1) Son of Thutmose I and Ahmose, general; 2) Brother of Nefertari, mayor of Thebes; 3) Son of Bekenptah, officer under the Ramessides.

Amenophis – According to Manetho Greek for Amenhotep and still often used in this sense; philologically correct for Amenemope.

Amenti – Realm of the Dead, cf Duat.

Ammit, Ammut – Chimera, destroyer of the hearts of the dead who were sinners. Goddess called Devouress of the Dead, who sits at the weighing of the heart at the entrance to the underworld.

Amratian – Middle pre-dynastic period, 3550 to 3400.

Amulets – Good luck charms, often in the form of hieroglyphs

Amun – Amun is the most important and powerful of all the Egyptian gods in ancient Egyptian history. Amun, whose name means '**hidden**', was originally worshipped locally in Thebes. Among all the Egyptian gods and goddesses, Amun is considered the most important. He is also referred to as a creator god, with generations of pharaohs adopting him as their patron deity. He was declared King of the Gods, with many temples erected bearing his name, such as those found in Karnak and Luxor. Amun's title has also been combined with that of the sun god Ra to form Amun-Ra – the almighty god of the sun and creation.

Amunet – Amunet was a fertility goddess.

Anat – Anat was a goddess of fertility, sexual love, hunting, and war of Canaanite.

Anch, ankh – Symbol of enduring life, its hieroglyph was occasionally worn as an amulet.

Anchesenamen, Anchesenamun, Ankhesenamen, Ankhesenamun, Ankhesenaten, Ankhesenpaaten – Wife of Tutankhamen, 18th dynasty.

Anchnesmerire, Ankhnesmeryre – Queen, the mother of Pepi II.

Anhur – Anhur was a foreign god of war and hunting, worshipped in Thinis.

Ankhmahor – 6th dynasty Vizier.

Ankhtifi – Nomarch in Upper Egypt.

Ant-fish – A mythological fish that accompanies the boat of Ra at sunrise.

Anubis, Anpu, Khenty-Imentiu, Hermanubis – Jackal/dog-headed god of the underworld and necropolis, the conductor of souls. Anubis is believed to be the one who embalmed Osiris, the first ever mummy.

The work of Anubis is said to form the basis of the Egyptian mummification process. As an early Egyptian god, he was worshipped as the ultimate god of the dead. As the number of Egyptian gods and goddesses increased, Osiris took this mantle. Ultimately, Anubis is widely considered as the god of embalming and mummification. During the final judgement, when death arrives, Anubis guides the deceased to the Scales of Ma'at. There, he oversees the weighing of the deceased's heart, balanced against the feather of Ma'at.

Anuket – Anuket was an ancient Egyptian goddess of the Nile.

Apep – Apep was regarded as an ancient spirit of evil and destruction, the deification of darkness and chaos.

Apis, Serapis, Osiris-Apis – A bull sacred to Osiris, who symbolises fertility, venerated at Memphis.

Apophis, Apopis, Apep – The serpent of Chaos.

Apotropaic – Having the power to avert evil.

Artaxerxes – Two Persian kings and Egyptian pharaohs of the 27th dynasty.

Ashur-Uballit – King of Assyria and contemporary of Akhenaten.

Astarte – A Syrian goddess, whose name is found occasionally in Egyptian inscriptions.

Atef – The crown worn by Osiris.

Aten, Aton – The sun disk and unique god of Akhenaten. Also known as Aton, the original aspect of Ra.

Atmu – An early name of the solar deity worshipped at Heliopolis.

Atum – Atum was known as the god of creation.

Ay – Merneferre, pharaoh of the 18th dynasty. Vizier of Tutankhamun.

Ba – Spiritual force such as an anonymous divinity. Manifestation of a god. The eternal forces of a human that is depicted in tombs as a bird with a human head.

Ba'ah, Seba-djai – The planet Venus.

Baal – Baal was a god of thunder.

Bai, Bay – Chancellor of Ramses Siptah, 19th dynasty.

Bakenkhons, Bakenkhonsu, Bekenkhonsu – The High Priest of Amen under Ramses II; it has been said he was the father of Nefertari.

Banebdjedet – The ram god of Lower Egypt.

Bast, Bastet, Ubasti, Pasht – Cat goddess. The goddess of the home.

Bastet is the daughter of Ra. She had a huge cult following in the city of Bubastis in the Nile delta. The goddess Bastet was depicted as a lioness. She was often associated with vengeance, ferocity and war. Through time, Bastet bore the less aggressive and sacred character of a domestic cat. Cats were treated as holy creatures, and were often mummified in death.

Bat – A goddess in the form of a cow, merged with Hathor.

Bau – Messenger or appearance of a deity.

Bes – A squat, grotesque goddess, Bes was the protector of pregnant women, children and households. She was usually depicted as a dwarf with an over-large head, small stumpy legs and an altogether ugly appearance.

Besa – A spirit of the corn.

Biridiya – Ruler of Megiddo and contemporary of Akhenaten.

Book of the Dead – Also referred to as The Book of Going Forth by Day. It is a collection of magical writings that was placed in tombs with the aim of helping the deceased in the afterlife.

Burnaburiash – Kassite king of Babylonia and contemporary of Akhenaten.

Cambyses, Kambyses – Persian king, conqueror of Egypt and founder of the 27th dynasty.

Canopic jars – The vessels containing the inner organs of the deceased person; generally there were four, in the form of the sons of Horus.

Cartonnage – Expression used by Egyptologists for the masks and coffins made of cardboard-like materials. Also referred to as a mummy mask.

Cartouche – The name of a pharaoh in hieroglyphs surrounded by an oval band denoting eternity.

Cataract – Rapids, waterfall. The first Nile cataract was Egypt's southern border.

Choachyte – Priest in charge of the cult of the dead who, for a fee, carried out the role of the undertaker.

Cippus – Amulet or stela showing Horus triumphing over dangerous beasts.

Coffin texts – Magical writings or spells written on wooden coffins to direct the souls of the dead beyond the dangers and perils of the afterlife.

Crook, heka – Originally a shepherd's staff, it became a symbol of power carried by pharaohs and high officials.

Cult temple – Temple for the worship of a God.

Darius – Two Persian kings and Egyptian pharaohs (27th dynasty).

Decans – 36 star constellations, each rising above the horizon at sunrise for ten days every year, used by the ancient Egyptian calendar.

Demotic – The last stage of development of the ancient Egyptian script.

Dendarah, Denderah – Site of Hathor's main temple.

Deshret – 1) The red crown of Lower Egypt; 2) The red land, i.e. the desert

Dionysus – Greek god, identified with Osiris.

Djed pillar – Hieroglyph often carried as an amulet, linked to represent the backbone of Osiris.

Djehuti, Thoth – 1) God of knowledge and wisdom, moon god, identified with Hermes Trismegistus by the Greeks; 2) Scribe, general and viceroy under Thutmose III.

Djoser, Zoser – Old Kingdom pharaoh, 3rd dynasty.

Duat – The Realm of the Dead, populated by the deceased who have become stars.

Dynasty – Line of hereditary rulers.

Early dynastic – Historic period 3050 to 2600 BCE, also called Naqada IIIA1 to IIIC1.

El Amarna, Al Amarna, Akhetaten – Capital of Egypt under Akhenaten, 18th dynasty.

Ennead – A group of nine deities, such as the Ennead of Heliopolis.

False door – Symbolic door for the *ka*. Painted or carved on a tomb wall through which the *ka* could enter and leave at will.

Flail, flagellum (from Latin flagrum, scourge), nekhekh, nekhakha – A flail carried by the pharaoh symbolizing his power; attribute of Osiris and Min.

Four Sons of Horus – Four gods in Egyptian religion, who were essentially the personifications of the containers for the organs of the deceased pharaohs.

Funerary offerings – Bread, wine, beer and other useful items for the wellbeing of the *ka*. The offerings were not always physical, but provided magically, or through inscriptions and pictures in the tomb.

Geb, Keb – Earth god, the father of Osiris. His parents were Shu, the god of the air, and Tefnet, goddess of the rain. His sister and wife was Nut, goddess of the sky. Geb is often depicted as dark brown (the colour of the flood plains), or green (the colour of vegetation). It is said that his loud laughter is the cause of earthquakes. He produced Osiris, Seth, Isis and Nepthys.

Gerzean – Late pre-dynastic and protodynastic periods, 3400 to 3050 BCE, divided into Early Gerzean, 3400 to 3300 BCE; Middle Gerzean, 3300 to 3200 BCE; Late Gerzean, 3200 to 3050 BCE.

God's father – A priest of intermediate rank.

Grave goods – Equipment left in the tomb to provide what was needed for the afterlife.

Griffin – A chimera with the body of a lion and the head of a falcon, symbol of the victorious.

Hah – Personification of eternity that props up the heavens.

Hapi, Hapy – 1) God of the Nile; 2) One of the Four Sons of Horus. Hapi was the ancient Egyptian god of the Nile, depicted as green-skinned, with a woman's breasts, representing the fertility and life-giving resources of the river. The ancient Egyptians would pray to Hapi to ensure that the annual inundations or floods would bring sufficient water to their fields and there would be a plentiful harvest. The Egyptians worshipped Hapi more than any other Egyptian gods and goddesses due to the importance of the River Nile in Egyptian society.

Hapiru, Apiru, Habiru – Nomadic asiatics of the second millennium BCE, often considered outlaws.

Harakhte – God.

Harmakhis – Horus on the horizon – the rising or setting sun.

Harem – An institution run by the pharaoh's first wife for the benefit of the pharaoh's wives and female relatives.

Haroeris – The mature Horus, with the capacity for ruling.

Harpocrates – The immature Horus. The child was the son of Isis and Osiris and often depicted on the lap of his mother Isis and with a sidelock of youth and sucking his fingers.

Hathor – Goddess of sky, love, mirth, beauty and fertility. Hathor is one of the oldest Egyptian goddesses, dating to pre-dynastic times. She is often depicted as a cow, or a woman with a cow's head, or a woman with the horns of a cow and a solar disc on her head. Her major temple is at Dendera.

Hatmehyt – Hatmehyt was an Egyptian goddess of fish, originally a deification of the Nile River.

Hatshepsut, Hatshepsowe – Female pharaoh, 18th dynasty.

Hauhet – One of the oldest Egyptian gods in ancient Egyptian history; the deification of eternity in the Ogdoad.

Hedjet, nefer-hedjet – The white crown of Upper Egypt.

Heka – The god of magic and medicine.

Hekt – The frog-headed goddess of birth.

Heliopolis – Main temple of the sun god Re.

Hemaka – Royal sealbearer (chancellor).

Hepu – Vizier under Thutmose IV.

Hepuseneb – First prophet of Amen under Hatshepsut.

Heqa – Crook, symbol of pharaonic authority.

Heqat, Heqet, Hekt, Hekat, Heket – Goddess of childbirth , creation and fertility, often seen in the form of a frog.

Her-desuf – A form of Horus.

Her-ka-pet – The planet Saturn.

Heru-deshret – The planet Mars.

Her-wepes-tawy – The planet Jupiter.

Hesire – Overseer over the royal scribes under Djoser (3rd dynasty), physician and dentist.

Hieratic – Cursive writing of hieroglyphs.

Hieroglyphics – Ancient Egyptian writing using stylized pictures (hieroglyphs).

Hittites – People of Hatti.

Hor – 1) Hor, pharaoh, probably 13th dynasty; 2) Hor, priest during the Late Period; 3) Hor, mountain in northern Canaan.

Horakhti – The Horizon-Horus.

Horbaf – Son of Khufu (4th dynasty), vizier.

Hordjedef, Djedefhor – Son of Khufu (4th dynasty).

Horemheb – New Kingdom general and pharaoh, 18th dynasty.

Horus, Hor, Heru, Hru – Sun god, son of Isis and Osiris, originally the sky god. Horus is one of the more important Egyptian gods. He is usually depicted as a man with the head of a falcon, or sometimes as a falcon as well. He is also depicted as a falcon encircling the head of the pharaoh with his wings. When the evil god Set murdered Osiris, it was Horus who avenged his father and killed Set. Horus is also features in the http://www.nekhebet.com/m_mummies.html- judgment final judgment. Once the deceased passes the weighing of the scales, it is Horus who leads the deceased to the underworld.

House of Life – Repositories for knowledge in temples.

Huh – Huh was one of the oldest Egyptian gods in ancient Egyptian history, the deification of eternity in the Ogdoad.

Ihy – Ihy was a child god and was also the god of music and musicians.

Ikhernofret – The chancellor under Senusret III.

Imhotep – High official under Djoser, who was later deified.

Intef, Antef, Inyotef – Pharaohs of the 11th dynasty.

Isfet – Disorder, chaos, opposed to Ma'at.

Isis, Auset, Aset, Ast – Goddess of motherhood, fertility and nature and consort of Osiris. The greatest of goddesses. The Egyptian goddess Isis was the sister and wife of Osiris and mother of Horus. Her cult was by far the largest of all the Egyptian gods, reaching into Europe. Isis is commonly depicted as a seated queen suckling and cradling the baby Horus. This symbolism was said to be the influence for the notion of the Virgin Mary and the baby Jesus. In addition, she can be depicted with either a throne or a vulture on top of her head. When her husband was killed by their brother Set, it was she who collected the dismembered body parts of Osiris and re-formed the body using bandages, thus laying the foundation for the ancient Egyptian practice of mummifying the deceased. She was able to bring Osiris back to life, thus introducing the concept of resurrection.

Judgment of the Dead – The decision by the gods on the afterlife of a person before them.

Justified – True of voice, a dead person judged favourably.

Ka – The immortal part of a being that requires nourishment, coming into existence together with the being: the life force. Created at the time of birth by the god Khnum, who fashioned beings on his potter's wheel, before placing them inside their mother. The *ka* could be released during life in dreams, but was finally released at death. Symbolised by a pair of upraised arms.

Kadashman Enlil – King of Babylon and contemporary of Amenhotep III.

Kamutef – Bull of his Mother. Name of the ithyphallic, self-created Amen and Min.

Kanofer – Architect under Khasekhemwy (2nd dynasty), possibly Imhotep's father.

Karnak, Al Karnak – Modern village that occupies the northern half of pharaonic Thebes.

Kauket – One of the oldest Egyptian gods in ancient Egyptian history, the deification of the primordial concept of darkness.

Kawab – Son of Khufu (4th dynasty).

Kenbet – Judicial commission or court.

Khafre, Chafre, Chefren – Old Kingdom pharaoh, 4th dynasty.

Khaemwaset – Son of Ramses II, high priest of Ptah.

Khamudi, Chamudi, Apepi II – Hyksos king.

Khekheperre-sonbu – Priest (Admonitions).

Khepera – The rising sun, god of resurrection.

Khepresh, Kheperesh – The blue crown.

Khepri – God of creation, the movement of the sun, life and resurrection.

Khnum – Ram-headed God of the Nile.

Khons, Khonsu – 1) Moon god, son of Amen and Mut, his main temple was at Karnak; 2) Called To: First prophet of Menkheperra under Ramses II.

Khufu, Cheops – Old Kingdom pharaoh, 4th dynasty.

Kohl – Black eyeliner.

Kuk – One of the oldest Egyptian gods in ancient Egyptian history, the deification of the concept of darkness.

KV – Term used by archaeologists together with a number to identify tombs in the Valley of the Kings.

Labayu – Ruler of Shechem, contemporary of Akhenaten.

Lector priest – Priest reading ritual texts at cult ceremonies and funerals. He wore a broad white sash across his chest.

Lower Egypt – Geographical term for the land around the Nile delta, from modern Cairo to the Mediterranean coast.

LPH – Life, prosperity, health: wish for wellbeing, added after the names of pharaohs, prosperity should rather be soundness.

Luxor – Modern village that occupies the southern half of ancient Thebes.

Maahes – Maahes was a solar war god of ancient Egypt in the form of a lion.

Maa-kheru – True of voice, justified. Used for: 1) the winning party in a trial; 2) the dead whose heart weighed less than a feather.

Maat, Ma'at, Mayet – The goddess of truth, justice, world order, proper conduct. Together with her husband Thoth, Ma'at was there when the Ra created the world. Ma'at also symbolized the balance of creation. This balance has to be maintained or chaos will ensue and the world will plunge into chaos. Every pharaoh was given a mandate to rule as long as he pledged to follow Ma'at, and ensure that balance and justice was forever upheld. The goddess Ma'at plays a key role in the final judgement. It is in the Hall of Ma'at that the heart of the dead is weighed against the feather of Ma'at, to determine if they are eligible to enter the underworld. Ma'at is commonly depicted with an ostrich feather on her head, and with wings connected to her arms.

Mafdet – A goddess symbolizing judicial authority and the execution apparatus.

Mastaba – Large mud-brick, rectangular shaped superstructure built over tomb shafts.

Mehen – The serpent who protects Ra in the Duet.

Memphis, Mennefer, Mof – Old Kingdom capital of Egypt.

Men, Menes, Min – First pharaoh of the united kingdom according to Herodotus.

Menhit – Menhit was the goddess of war origin from Nubia.

Menkaure, Mykerinos – Old Kingdom pharaoh, 4th dynasty.

Menkheperreseneb – High priest of Amon at Karnak, 18th dynasty.

Mentu – God of war.

Mentuhotep, Montuhotep – Four pharaohs of the 11th dynasty.

Meretseger – Meretseger was a cobra Goddess who was the protector and guardian of the Valley of the Kings. She lived on the mountains that dominate the Valley.

Mereruka – Vizier under Teti (6th dynasty), successor of Kagemni.

Meryre, Pepi I, Pepy I – Old Kingdom pharaoh, 6th dynasty.

Meryt-Amen – Daughter of Akhenaten and Queen Nefertiti.

Meskhenet – The goddess of childbirth, personification of the birthing stone, two bricks placed under the feet of the woman giving birth in a crouching position.

Middle Egypt – Geographical term that is applied to the area south of Luxor, especially sites around Beni Hasan and Tell el Armana.

Min – God of fertility and harvest.

Mortuary cult – The provision of regular funerary offerings for the eternal wellbeing of the deceased.

Mortuary priest – Person appointed to bring funerary offerings daily to tomb; known as the 'servant of the *ka*'.

Mortuary temple – Where the mortuary cult of a King was carried out.

Monthu – Monthu was the falcon-headed god of war.

Mummy – A preserved corpse, this can be through natural or artificial means. The latter involves removing all sources of moisture from the body and thoroughly drying the body.

Mut – Mut was the great mother goddess of Egypt: 1) Mother goddess, often equated with Isis; 2) Deceased with often malicious intentions. Venerated as the great divine mother, Mut was generally portrayed as a woman wearing a white and red crown, but she has also been known to be portrayed with the head or body of a vulture and as a cow because in the later period, she merged with Hathor.

Naos – The sanctuary with the divine statues.

Narmer – King, thought by many to have united Upper and Lower Egypt.

Natron – Carbonate salt mixture used in mummifying. Found in the western delta. It could also be used as a cleaning agent for washing clothes, bodies or cleaning teeth.

Naunet – Nun was the waters of chaos.

Nebamen, Nebamon, Nebamun – Chief of police in western Thebes under Thutmose IV and Amenhoteop III.

Nebwawi – High Priest of Osiris under Thutmose III.

Necho, Neco, Necos, Nekhau – Two pharaohs of the Late Dynastic Period, 26th dynasty.

Necropolis – City of the dead, cemetery.

Nefer – Amulet made of gold, good luck charm.

Neferkare, Pepi II, Pepy II – Old Kingdom pharaoh, 6th dynasty.

Nefertari, Nefertari-Mery-Mut – The main wife of Ramses II.

Nefertiti, Nefertete, Nofretete – The wife of Akhenaten.

Nefertum – Nefertum was an ancient sun God, who was considered to be an aspect of Atum.

Neferty – Prophet.

Neith – Neith was an ancient Goddess of war and weaving

Nekhbet – Goddess of Upper Egypt represented in the form of a vulture Nekhebet, also known as Nekhbet, is commonly pictured as a vulture holding an ankh. She is sometimes depicted with her wings spread protectively over the pharaoh. Nekhebet had a protective nature, being the protector goddess of mothers and children.

Nephthys, Nepthys, Nebt-Het – The wife of Seth. Goddess, protective goddess of the dead. She was the sister of Osiris, Isis and Set, and the wife of Set. Nephthys is associated with her sister Isis and helping her with many things. She helped Isis gather the various parts of Osiris' body after Set had dismembered him. She also assisted Isis in delivering babies. She is often seen together with Osiris and Isis, ruling the underworld. Nephthys was depicted as a woman with a basket and a house on top of her head.

Nepra – A spirit of the corn.

Nitocris, Nitokris – Daughter of Psammetic I, 26th dynasty, Wife of the God Amen.

NK – New Kingdom.

Nomarch – Ruler of a Nom.

Nub – Gold.

Nun – Primordial god of water and fertility, often depicted as a green or blue man.

Nut – Goddess of the sky. Nut was the daughter of Shu, the Egyptian god of air, and Tefnut, goddess of water. She was also the sister and wife of Geb, god of the earth. She was commonly depicted as a naked woman arching over the earth, with her hands and feet touching the ground. Her body is usually sky-colored and filled with stars. She is also sometimes depicted as a cow. Some stories tell of Nut swallowing the sun in the evening, and giving birth to it in the morning. Nut is well known for being the mother of some of the most important Egyptian Gods: Osiris, Isis, Set and http://www.nekhebet.com/r_gods 2.html - nephthys Nephthys. The story of Nut mentions the sun god Ra forbidding her to bear any children for fear of them taking his throne. So Nut sought the help of the wise god Thoth and ultimately gave birth to her four children.

Ogdoad – The eight primeval gods of creation: Nun and Naunet, Kuk and Kauket, Huh and Hauhet, Amen and Amaunet.

OK – Old Kingdom.

On, Heliopolis – Main temple of the sun god Re.

Opening of the Mouth – The ceremony performed for a deceased person.

Osiris, Asr, Ausar – God of Duat, consort of Isis. Osiris was the god of the dead and vegetation. He is usually referred to as god of the afterlife. Osiris is one of the most important Egyptian gods, having a cult following that grew beyond Egypt's borders. Modern-day Egypt still celebrates festivals dedicated to him. Osiris is usually depicted as a mummy wearing the Atef crown with a crook and flail in his hands. Osiris became the king of the dead and the judge of the underworld. Egyptians viewed him as being triumphant over death; every pharaoh would be Osiris after death, while he was the embodiment of Horus when alive. Osiris was often painted with green skin, symbolizing new growth and renewal.

Pabi – Ruler of Lachish, contemporary of Akhenaten.

Pakhet – Pakhet was the Egyptian goddess of war.

Paser – 1) Viceroy under Ay and Horemheb; 2) Mayor and vizier under Sethi I and Ramses II.

Pepi – Two Old Kingdom pharaohs, 6th dynasty: 1) Pepi I, Pepy I, Meryre, 2) Pepi II, Pepy II, Neferkare, Son of Pepi.

Per nefer – House of beauty or good house. Place where part of the purification and mummification procedures or rituals took place.

Pesesh-kaf – Ceremonial instrument used in the Opening of the Mouth ceremony.

Pharaoh – Great house, or the house of the king. Also a king of Egypt.

Phoenix – Mythological bird.

Piankhi, Piye – Pharaoh of the Late Dynastic Period, 25th dynasty.

Pre-dynastic – Prehistoric period, 5500 to 3050 BCE.

Prehirwonnef – Son of Ramesses II and Queen Nefertari.

Proto-dynastic – Period 3200 to 3050, also called Late Gerzean.

Prophet – Servant of the god and head priest.

Psammetichos, Psammetic, Psamtek, Psamtik – Three pharaohs, 26th dynasty.

Pshent – The double crown of the united Egypt.

Ptach, Ptah – The creator-god and the patron deity of crafts and craftsmanship. Ptah was usually depicted as a mummified figure with his hands protruding through the bandaging to hold a staff with the symbols of dominion and stability.

Ptah – Creator god of Memphis. It was Ptah whom the sem priest emulated at the Opening of the Mouth, for Ptah was believed to have carried out a similar task on the gods at the time of their creation.

Ptahhotep – Vizier under Djedkare (5th Dynasty).

Pyramid – Monumental burial place for kings between the 3rd and 12th dynasty.

Pyramid texts – Texts or spells carved inside the pyramids concerning the afterlife of the deceased during the fifth and sixth dynasty.

Pyramidion – Capstone of a pyramid.

Qa'a – Last pharaoh of the first dynasty.

Qebehsenuef, Kebhsenuf – One of the four sons of Horus.

Qenbet – Judicial court.

Qetesh – – Qetesh was a goddess of ecstasy and sexual pleasure, originally from Syria.

Rameses, Ramesis, Ramesses, Ramses, Ramsis – Eleven pharaohs reigning during the New Kingdom, 19th and 20th dynasty.

Ramose – 1) Vizier under Amenhotep III and Amenhotep IV; 2) Vizier under Ramses II.

Re, Ra – Sun god, the most important Egyptian god. Ra represented the creative force of the sun. Many myths credit Ra to be the first of the gods, creating the world from a watery chaos. As the sun god, Ra is often depicted as a hawk-headed man with the solar disc on his head. He is also commonly pictured riding a boat. Ra will sail this boat into the underworld in the evening. Every night Ra has to overcome many challenges, the most difficult of which is the great serpent Apep. If he succeeds, he will be able to progress beyond the underworld and into the land of the living in the morning.

Rekhmire – Mayor and vizier under Thutmose III and Amenhotep II.

Reserve heads – Old Kingdom sculptures found in tombs at Giza, considered by many to represent true portraits of the dead.

Resheph – Resheph was a god of war and thunder, originally from Syria.

Rock-cut tomb – Method begun during the Middle Kingdom of excavating tombs from solid rock. The tombs in the Valley of the Kings are a good example.

Rosetau, Rasetjau – Place in the afterlife, the underworld.

Sabgu – The planet Mercury.

Sah – The constellation of Orion, associated with Osiris.

Sakkara, Saqqara – Burial ground near Memphis.

Sarcophagus – (Greek sarx + phagos, flesh eating) stone coffin.

Satis – Satis is the goddess of the Nile and fertility.

Scarab – 1) Dung beetle, 2) Amulet in the form of a dung beetle.

Sechmet, Sekhmet – The Goddess of love and protection. Sekhmet was a powerful and destructive force, and was often depicted as a woman with the head of a lioness. She is also associated with red, the colour of blood. During her reign as pharaoh, the people of Egypt became independent and therefore disloyal to her. So it was in retribution that Ra created Sekhmet to attack the people to teach them a lesson. Sekhmet was too successful in her task. Each day, the fields ran red with the blood of her victims. Feeling some remorse for creating this force of destruction, Ra tried to stop Sekhmet, but she continued killing. Ultimately, to stop the carnage, Ra disguised beer as blood and got Sekhmet drunk, so she was unable to continue with her task.

Sed Festival, Heb Sed – Celebration of the 30th anniversary of a pharaoh's rule, sometimes celebrated after a shorter time period.

Seker – Seker was the Memphite god of the dead.

Sekh tent – A form of temporary structure erected at the tomb where the final funerary rites take place.

Selk – The scorpion-goddess.

Sem priest – Wearing a leopard skin garment he is associated with the funerary ritual and the Opening of the Mouth ceremony.

Senmut, Senemut – Minister and favourite of Queen Hatshepsut.

Senusert, Senusret, Senwosret, Sesostris – Three Middle Kingdom pharaohs, 12th dynasty.

Serdab – Old Kingdom underground funerary chapel or burial shaft that contains a statue of the deceased.

Serket – Serket was the goddess of scorpion.

Serpopards – Long-necked chimera.

Seshat – Goddess, her name means 'female scribe'. Seshat is an ancient Egyptian goddess of wisdom, knowledge, and writing from Lower Egypt.

Set, Seth – The god of chaos, evil, storms, desert and darkness. Brother of Osiris, Isis and Nepthys, whose husband he was. The personification of evil. Set is most commonly portrayed as a man with a black coloured demonic head, resembling that of an aardvark. Originally, Set was the patron god of the pharaohs of Lower (Northern) Egypt, as Horus was the patron god of the pharaohs of Upper (Southern) Egypt. Some pharaohs incorporated Set's name into their own. However, as the cult of Osiris grew larger and the story of Osiris's murder grew more popular, Set was depicted as being more evil and chaotic. He would become associated with barren deserts and thunderstorms. After Set was defeated by Horus, he was banished from Egypt, and spent his time protecting Ra on his nightly voyage through the underworld.

Setau – Viceroy of Kush under Ramses II.

Setep – Ceremonial instrument used in the opening of the mouth ceremony.

Shabti, Shawabti – Mummy-style statuette of the deceased that was placed in tombs to do manual labour.

Shepseskaf – King (4th dynasty), son of Menkaure.

Sheshonk, Sheshonq – Five pharaohs reigning during the 3rd Intermediate Period, 22th and 23th dynasty.

Shezmu – Shezmu was the ancient Egyptian demonic god of slaughter, execution, blood and wine.

Shu – The Egyptian god of air.

Shuwardata – Ruler of Keilah, contemporary of Akhenaton.

Snefru, Sneferu, Snofru – Old Kingdom Pharaoh, 4th dynasty.

Solar boat, ship, barque – Boat used by the sun god to cross the heavens.

Sobek – Sobek is the crocodile god or Lord of Faiyum Oasis from Faiyum.

Sokar – The hawk-headed god of the dead. When fused with Ptah (Ptah-Sokar) he appears in the form of a misshapen dwarf, and is then looked upon as a god of resurrection.

Sopdet/Soqdet – Soqdet was one of the important goddesses of the star Sirius.

Sphinx – Statue with lion's body and human or animal head.

Stela, stele – Monumental stone slab with inscriptions or carvings. A memorial to a dead person (gravestone), a commemoration of a victory or a major event, or even a formal decree.

Tadu-heba, Tadukhipa – Daughter of Tushratta, married to Amenhotep III.

Tatenen – Tatenen, the god of Rising Earth, who identified with creation.

Ta-urt – The hippopotamus goddess of birth.

Tauret, Taweret, Tauwret – A fertility goddess.

Tawaret – Tawaret was the Egyptian goddess who protected women during pregnancy and childbirth.

Tefnut – Lioness-headed goddess of dew, rain and moisture. Twin-sister of Shu. The two form the constellation Gemini.

Tepu-yn – A spirit of the corn.

Teti – 6th dynasty pharaoh.

Thebes, No, Waset, Wese – The New Kingdom capital of Egypt and centre of the Amen cult.

Thoth, Thot, Toth, Tehuti, Djehuti – The ultimate god of wisdom, his main temple was at Hermopolis, Hermes. **The** god of writing, knowledge, time, fantasy, speaking, inventions and moon. Thoth, the ibis-headed god of wisdom, was also associated with the moon. He is another of the more important Egyptian gods, featuring in almost all the myths.

Thuthmose, Thutmose, Thutmosis, Tuthmosis – Four New Kingdom pharaohs, 18th dynasty.

Tiye – Wife of Amenhotep III, daughter of Yuya and Tuyu, mother of Akhenaten.

Triad – Three related gods – the Theban Triad, the Triad of Abydos, the Triad of Memphis.

Tushratta – King of Mitanni, first half of the 14th century BCE.

Tutanchamen, Tutanchamun, Tutankhamen, Tutankhaten, Tutankhamun – A New Kingdom pharaoh, 18th dynasty.

Two lands – The united land of Upper and Lower Egypt, since the New Kingdom also referred to as Kemet.

Tyet, Tet, The Blood of Isis, The Buckle of Isis – Symbol associated with Isis, amulet made of red semi-precious stone.

Uazet – Goddess of Lower Egypt.

Udjat, Wedjat – The eye of Horus, amulet.

Unas, Weni, Wenis – Old Kingdom pharaoh, 5th dynasty.

Upper Egypt – Southern Egypt, generally referring to locations between Luxor and Aswan, it occasionally includes middle Egypt.

Upuaut, Wepwawet – Guardian god in the shape of a canine – jackal-god of Siut.

Uraeus – Symbolic cobra, part of the headdress of pharaohs and Gods.

Ushabti – Small wooden or glazed stone mummiform figures that were placed in tombs to undertake work on behalf of the deceased, and who may be called upon to perform tasks in the afterlife. Also referred to as Shawabti.

Userkaf – First king of the fifth dynasty.

Valley of the Kings – The pharaonic burial site near Thebes during the New Kingdom, modern name for ancient 'The Great and Majestic Necropolis of the Millions of Years of the Pharaoh in the West of Thebes, otherwise known as The Great Field'.

Valley of the Queens – Burial site of queens near Thebes.

Valley Temple – Place on the Nile edge where the king's body was received for its final rites before being transported via the connecting causeway to the pyramids.

Vizier – The king's chief minister, ambassador, supreme civil and criminal judge.

Wabet – Place where part of the purification or mummification rites took place.

Wadjet, wedjat, uzat – The serpent goddess and the lunar eye of Horus. Often seen in amulet form to protect from the evil eye. Wadjet was worshiped as a cobra and was often included in royal insignia as a symbol of sovereignty over Egypt. She was the protector of the living Horus – the pharaoh. She was generally painted as being poised to strike at any potential enemy of the pharaoh. Often depicted as a woman with two snake heads.

Wadjet Eye – The left eye of Horus, restored by the god Thoth. Symbolising the power of healing.

Wassceptre – The symbol of well-being and happiness.

Weni, Uni – 6th dynasty official, governor of Upper Egypt, who served under a number of different pharaohs.

Wepwawet – Originally a war god whose name means 'opener of the roads', Wepwawet is portrayed as a canine creature that is claimed to be a jackal, a wolf, or an ordinary dog.

Xerxes – A Persian king and pharaoh of Egypt (585–546).

Yarsu – Often identified with Merneptah Siptah's chancellor, Bay, in the 19th dynasty.

Yuya – A high official under Thutmose IV, husband of Tuyu.

Zaphnathpaaneah, Zaphnath-paaneah – According to the Bible, the Egyptian name of Joseph.

Chapter 1

Death in the Desert Sands

It seems appropriate to begin our research into the curse of the pharaoh's tombs by looking at the most legendary and infamous curse of them all, that of the boy pharaoh, Tutankhamun. Since 1922 tales of this curse have circulated in different formats across all aspects of the media. Each time the tale is retold it seems that further embellishment occurs, at times making it more unbelievable and preposterous. Most writers who reiterate tales of the curse simply recount the mysterious deaths of various people associated with the tomb opening, from across the globe. The basis of the curse has undoubtedly been lost in translation, and with the passage of time and the addition of unreliable glorified testimony it has been transformed from a believable and actual matter, to a more obscure and supernatural, and therefore unbelievable, subject. Modern-day writers and researchers tend to accept that a few of the deaths were little more than curious coincidences, and Egyptologists tend to steer well away from the topic of curses because of its less than acceptable academic standing. Thus as a serious subject it tends to be ignored, since it is regarded as so bizarre and belonging to the realm of the supernatural. Despite this, there is huge interest in the subject of Egyptian curses: one need only look at the number of films that have been produced (at the last count I listed twenty-four). In 2011 I carried out a survey among visitors to the British Museum, asking one simple question: *'Do you believe in the Curse of the Pharaohs or the Curse of the Mummy and Egyptian Tombs?'* In total I asked 1,000 people visiting the museum, over the period of one week. I offered no prompting or guidance. The results were illuminating. Some 98 per cent of people stated that they believed in the curse, with just 2 per cent claiming that they didn't believe in anything supernatural or inexplicable. No one asked for any further explanation of what the 'Curse of the Pharaohs, or the Curse of the Mummy or Egyptian Tombs' might mean. They had their own perception of the subject and clearly all imagined it to relate to supernatural sources, therefore its credibility instantly becomes dubious. The survey was deliberately multi-cultural, showing that belief in the curse isn't solely a Western phenomenon. I recall a similar public attitude when I was carrying out research into the Loch Ness Monster: the instant it was mentioned in public, people withdrew from any discussion about why they visited the loch, and why they stood watching, looking out over its waters, occasionally for several hours, scanning its surface through binoculars. The subject is an unknown and inexplicable quantity, so it becomes a taboo subject because people believe that being associated with such beliefs creates an unwanted stigma, and that those who delve into such mysteries must be eccentric in their own rational beliefs.

I'm used to having a curious label attached to my research into matters such as the Loch Ness Monster and curses. However, it is my belief that we should treat the unknown with respect, and fully research it until, in the words of Sherlock Holmes 'When you have eliminated the impossible, whatever remains, however improbable, must be the truth.' Sir Arthur Conan Doyle, who created Sherlock Holmes, first used these lines in his February 1890 work, 'The Sign of Four'. Conan Doyle was an ardent believer in the supernatural, including Egyptian curses, so the mysterious path we walk in search of answers to the great and often dark mysteries of the world is not a unique one! In 2009, during a research visit to Egypt, I dedicated much of my time initially to study in the Cairo museum, examining records of ancient documents and discussing the great pharaohs and curses with many scholars, before travelling to other areas of historical interest across the region. I visited dozens of tombs, worked on archaeological dig sites, and spoke with countless 'experts' in Egyptology along the way. My sole aim was to investigate curses, since this clearly interests many others across the globe. One thing became evident during my research and investigations: very few people feel comfortable discussing Egyptian curses, and most pass over the subject as though it doesn't exist and is of no importance. When first mentioned in conversation it usually arouses a nervous titter, accompanied by an uncomfortable reaction of the eyes, which dart left to right, up and down, in the vain hope that the subject will be dropped from conversation. Yet privately the public are interested in such matters. Whenever I am asked to give a presentation or talk on the subject of Egyptian curses I do so to packed audiences.

Upon returning home to England I received a typed letter from Egypt. It was from a person who was clearly well educated and knowledgeable. Without psycho-analysing that individual any further, the contents of the letter are disclosed here for the first time.

My grandfather was a man named Asim, he was an intelligent and learned man who was able to speak with and understand visiting Westerners. He learned to speak English through his daily interaction with such people. My grandfather was a person whom others would call upon for advice and assistance, he was seen by many as clever and sensible, not one to elaborate or extinguish the truth, he was sombre, honest and above all, genuine. My father told me how Asim would read as many English-speaking books (of all kinds) that he could; he was especially interested in those that discussed European history. He wasn't one to waste time on matters of no consequence, he cherished life and wanted to embrace as much of it as he could. He would say that knowledge was power and positive knowledge would ultimately help the world develop into a better place. I remember him saying that money and greed was the cause of much pain and anguish among people all over the world, he was a great believer in first, and foremost, providing for his family, caring for them and being able to support those he most cherished.

Because he was so literate, he was well connected when it came to finding employment and in gaining managerial positions on things like archaeological digs. The manual workforce that supported the archaeologists' searches across Egypt came from local communities; it was paid but extremely hard work in difficult conditions. It isn't really expressed too much as being this way but Asim described it as being similar

3

to slave labour. On many digs the workforce lived in small camps near to where excavations were taking place, the conditions were dreadful, food and drinks were available at set times only, the sanitary conditions weren't great either. When the dig for Tutankhamun began, this was long before the tomb was discovered, Asim was among those Egyptians selected to aid excavations. The following letter is in his words not mine or those of anyone else. I am sir, your obedient servant Habbi

A second, incomplete letter was enclosed. It read:

Working in the desert wasn't good for the soul or the mind, and it wasn't good for the body. It was an expensive pastime and the archaeologists received monetary support from wealthy overseas benefactors, they were also restricted to strict timescales to carry out excavations in the Valley of the Kings and elsewhere, it was great pressure to deliver which they endured. In turn that pressure was put upon the workers some of whom would suffer as a result of the dismal moods of the archaeologists, this was more obvious when the benefactors came to visit excavation sites, there was an expectancy to deliver success, and not, as so happened in many instances, just desert sand!

Workers were pushed to clear rubble and dig throughout the day, sometimes in searing sunshine and with no rest. The one thing I liked about Carter and Carnarvon was their ability to wander through excavation areas and communicate with the workforce, they seemed to understand how grueling it could be and made every effort to keep all the men happy and fit and healthy. They gave regular breaks and changed routines to keep everyone alert and interested. Carnarvon liked to talk to the local workers, he would ask their opinions and sought advice on local knowledge and beliefs and customs. He understood the men's respect for the afterlife and their worries about what disturbing it could mean: it wasn't discussed as a curse, but as an evil act of revenge that came from the afterlife for entering that world through the tombs.

I can recall with great clarity the moment when the first step that led into the tomb of King Tutankhamun was discovered. Excavation sites were generally busy and hard-working places, where dozens of men were focused on the task in hand, for much of the time there was silence, then every so often when someone made a find there was much shouting and attention drawing to the area of the find. This was so that the archaeologists, who could not be everywhere at once, could be alerted to the find. The vast majority of finds were of small items of pottery so were easily uncovered and revealed. Yet when the first step of the tomb was found there was much more excited shouting, this was because it was obvious that it (the step) was part of a more substantial structure, within a few moments people were shouting, we have found it. For many minutes, work on the dig and in the entire area stopped, this was while the archaeologists visited and viewed the find. This time there was something very different about the atmosphere, the archaeologist dropped to his knees and with his hand, swept more sand clear. Carter arrived and removed further sand, I saw by the look in his eyes that the find was an important one. He shook the worker who made the discovery, by the hand and gave him a great hug, a huge cheer went up across the entire area of the dig. I heard Carter say that he couldn't be sure of the significance because it was simply a step, however, he believed it could only be one thing, the entrance to a tomb. There was much concern because most archaeologists believed the tomb of King Tutankhamun would be more prominent, yet secluded in its location, this stone step had been found very close to the tomb of Ramesses VI.

A different archaeologist, Theodore Davis, believed he had found the tomb of King Tutankhamun many years earlier, during his dig he discovered funerary artifacts that depicted the king's name, he stopped his excavations because he was so sure he had unearthed all there was to find and all that remained in the Valley of the Kings. Carter was convinced there was more and that the tomb of King Tutankhamun had not been discovered by Davis. A meeting of archaeologists was called in one of the tents, and the area surrounding the tent was guarded so that only those present could know what was being discussed. I was close by sharing some water with some workers when I was called to the tent, there was much excited talking taking place and I was asked along with two other men to get a message sent to Lord Carnarvon to notify him that Carter had found something. Carter had scribbled the message onto a piece of paper, he was insistent that we should not tell anyone else about it and that we were to inform Lord Carnarvon that he would update him with more definite news when he was able. As I was about to leave I received a message telling me to put together a team of workers and to go to the step and sift away sand and debris. Carter did not wish to miss anything during the clearance we had to work carefully but with some haste because he knew we were close to something important.

As the steps descended the more difficult it was for us to remove the sand because there was more of it, so more workers were drafted in to help remove it. It took days to clear twelve of the steps until we reached the upper part of a blocked entrance doorway. Carter was there observing everything and at night he had guards stand over the dig to ensure no one accessed it without his authority. It was late in the afternoon and he (Carter) looked closely at the upper part of the sealed door, he believed there would be a name or some other clue about what was inside. He found the impression of the Royal Necropolis and with that and from his belief of the design of the tomb doorway he believed this was a tomb that dated back to the 18th Dynasty. The excitement among many present at the dig site was clear, some workers urged Carter to proceed and enter, but many others, most of the men, asked him not do it while they were present in fear of the vengeance of the gods for entering this sacred place. Carter knew of the superstitions and dismissed them as nonsense. Many workers were openly sobbing and praying for their own and their families' safe-keeping.

Carter instructed us to fill in the steps until further notice, and he would place guards around the area to stop unauthorised entry. There was little more any of us could do as we were forced to wait for Lord Carnarvon to attend the site before it could again be uncovered, this time exposing the entire doorway. It was over two weeks before Carnarvon could to get to the Valley of the Kings, and the site was prepared for the final dig, the day Carnarvon and his daughter (Lady Evelyn Herbert) got there, we uncovered sixteen steps in total that led directly down to the foot of the sealed entrance doorway. Carter and some of his fellows were quickly examining the door, he called out that he had found seals that bore Tutankhamun's name. It was an incredible moment then suddenly Carter had everyone stop. He noticed that the tomb doorway had previously been broken through, he shouted that tomb robbers had been inside. There was a sense of dejection in his voice then he suddenly seemed elated. We were told this was because the tomb had been resealed thereby showing it had not been emptied. When the doorway was finally removed there was a general air of ill-feeling among many of the workers, not towards Carter or the archaeologists, but the concern that what they were part of was sinful and they would be punished by the underworld for such sacrilege.

Behind the door was a passage filled with rock, Carter instructed workers to clear the debris from the area. This was the first time anyone had set foot inside that tomb for 3,000 years and it was Egyptian workers who were the first inside during the clearance. A chain of men was formed as the rocks were passed from inside the passage and out of the dig area. I can still recall the smell that came from inside that passage, it was sweet and sickly, I could smell it from the top of the access staircase, I had no reason to enter the tomb and didn't want to, something felt wrong about it. Then, suddenly one of the workers inside the passage screamed out that the face of a black jackal or desert dog stared at him through the gloom, he was delirious, and after a few moments of manic screaming he fell to the floor in a deep faint. He was at once carried outside for air. I was surprised by the attitude of the archaeologists

7

who insisted that the man be immediately replaced and the clearance work continue, they did not seem to have any care for him. The worker never regained consciousness, he never saw his family again, the last thing he had claimed to see was a black jackal or dog snarling at him, he expired in the Valley of the Kings. An Egyptian doctor said later that the man had died of fright!

The clearance continued, and was about twelve feet along the passage when the two front workers, who were at the deepest point inside, both stopped working and ran out into the daylight. One of them, Imbram had the look of insanity about him, his eyes were wide open and bulging, his face white as death, he could not speak, he could only muster gurgling noises and he was shaking uncontrollably. The second worker, Fenzil, was also shaking, his entire body appeared to have gone into a seizure and his eyes were rolling in his head. He also claimed to see a tall black jackal/dog-headed man stood upright in the passageway, he said it possessed evil eyes and spoke without moving its mouth, it was snarling and warned both men to at once leave the tomb or unimaginable pains would be suffered by them and their family for all eternity. Imbram threw a rock at the creature, the rock flew through it into empty space. The threatening creature suddenly lunged towards him and grabbed hold of his hand, taking it in its mouth. Imbram screamed out in pain and in terror both men stumbled out of the tomb as quickly as they could. Lying on the desert sand, away from the tomb entrance, both men were delirious and shouted warnings to other local workers. Imbram was apparently the more damaged of the two men, he was taken away from the site and never recovered from the incident. He died several hours later.

The physician who examined him before he expired claimed to notice several lacerations on his right hand, he commented that it was his belief these had been caused by manual labour and the handling of heavy rocks. Fenzil survived for several days before his body painfully gave up after his lungs exploded! He was in a constant state of fever and talked

8

incessantly of death being at his side with the gods of the Duat (realm of the dead) tormenting his last living hours by torturing his mind with voices and images of violent death. He claimed the boy king (Tutankhamun) was angered by the intrusion of his tomb and had wished vengeance on those who violated his final resting place. In the final moments before his death, Fenzil suddenly became lucid and explained to his family that in the madness that prevailed through his illness, he spoke the truth, the jackal god was real and had damned him for eternity. He warned his family not to disrupt the peace of the tombs or they too would suffer as he had.

Howard Carter had been present at the time of the incidents and was kept informed of the ill workers' fate. He dismissed all suggestions that dead guardians of the underworld had risen and were protecting the tomb. He told key workers, such as myself, to promote calm and deny all talk of the afterlife and evil vengeful protectors of the tomb. Workers were told that should they be heard talking of such things on site or elsewhere they would be removed from the dig and immediately replaced. This ensured that control of the excavations was maintained by the lead archaeologists and that the workers did what was asked of them and no more. It was a very difficult situation because of the fear that existed, natural explanations were given for the deaths such as the men already suffering ill health. At no point was there was any thought given to stopping the clearance of the tomb, it seemed to me that the health of Egyptian workers was of secondary value, they were expendable.

Soon other strange unaccountable occurrences began to happen, and discontent gradually spread through the workforce as a common belief that the deaths were an act of vengeance from the gods of the Duat who protected this tomb. One worker close to the outer entrance doorway of the tomb refused to go any further into the passageway, he claimed to hear the wailing voices of the dead commanding the spirits of the underworld to rise. Two other men claimed to see the jackal/dog-headed god standing guard, growling and staring menacingly at them. It was only when archaeologists physically supported the clearance of the passageway that some order was restored, all the workforce was distracted by the singing of songs and this helped with the speed in which the passageway was cleared. The guards who watched over the tomb after darkness had fallen spoke of hearing voices coming from the passageway and inside the tomb, but when an archaeologist was called he dismissed this claim as wind whistling through the narrow chamber. Yet the guards claimed it was not the wind but the sounds of many people talking in a manner that they described as though they were speaking to the gods in prayer.

On the day when the tomb was finally opened there were many visitors who had gathered to witness the event. Instead of an air of great excitement about what was to be uncovered, there seemed to be an air of anticipation of what might be unleashed when the inside of the tomb was exposed. Nobody openly discussed the fact that we were disturbing the dead, which in any religion is not a good or proper thing to do, but this is what we were doing, this was Tutankhamun's final resting place, and here was assembled an audience of the wealthy and fortunate from around the globe, treating such sacrilege as though it were a form of entertainment. That was the first time I felt sadness in my heart, I felt I had betrayed Tutankhamun himself. After all it was through our efforts that the body of the dead king had been made so vulnerable, an object of curiosity. In my opinion it was anything but dignified, I understood the need to unveil our history, but this to many of us didn't feel as though history was of any importance, it was the valuables and the treasures that might be found within that brought such an attendance. I know those with genuine interest, such as Carter and Lord Carnarvon, were good decent people, and some of their fellows did care, it was those who came for a rare visit or to claim they had been inside the tomb. Those people were not all kindly or respectful of us or of the history. Some of those were as bad as the tomb robbers, they stole valuable artifacts from the sands as souvenirs, they treated workers with no respect, making unnecessary demands of them, many of them treated animals with more kindliness than Egyptian people. A good many of the original visitors who visited the tomb were ill prepared for the desert conditions, with clothing and attire that was better suited to Western cities, not the hot dry desert sun. Some suffered from the dangers of the exposure to such heat, exhaustion and fainting was common, as was sickness with the change of diet aiding the suffering. Many workers saw this as a warning from the gods and on more than one occasion tried to explain this to tomb visitors, but the language barrier prevented the accurate conveying of the workers real fear to Westerners.

While Egyptian workers were allowed access to the tomb under the strict supervision of archaeologists, the original workforce was slowly reduced in numbers as greater focus was upon the content of the tomb rather than external excavations. Three further deaths occurred to local Egyptians during this period, one was accepted as death through heart failure and over exertion, the man in question had been feeling unwell for several days, so this is hardly suspicious. However, the other two deaths were decidedly more sinister and had unnatural causes attached to them. Both victims (men) died independently of one another and, at different times, both had a madness forced upon them that wasn't previously known and therefore because of the spontaneity of its onset, was undeniably frightening to the men, and those who witnessed the onset of the madness. A situation occurred when some of the treasures were being removed from the tomb, the objects were carried by Egyptian workers out of the chambers, along the corridor and up the staircase into the daylight sun. Almost everything was recorded in registers and logs by Howard Carter, it was known that many smaller items were not recorded, such items were gifted (in some cases sold) to selected visitors, the handing over or sale was never conducted by Carter himself, but by some of his team.

A foreman of a workforce team that was helping to remove the artifacts observed such trading and dared to voice his concerns that dishonorable dealings were occurring in the Valley of the Kings. He warned Carter that he was disobeying the rules of Egypt and would arouse the displeasure of the gods that ruled the region. He accused Carter of being little better than a tomb robber. Naturally, Carter was agitated by such a suggestion and dismissed the man's opinion as being of no consequence, and further added that there were no gods ruling the Valley of the Kings, they were ancient inventions of the scribes, storytellers and writers that had been handed down from generation to generation, he told him they were nothing but fables, stories! He instructed the man to forget such nonsense and suggested that he was wrong in his idea that any artifact was leaving the tomb immorally. This wasn't a denial that objects were being sold, or given as gifts, it was more of a suggestion that those carrying out this trade had no morals, nor had those accepting or paying for the items. Carter added that nothing of any value had been lost throughout the excavations and that the workers witnessing any such trade must be working too hard, have exhaustion and misinterpreted matters. The worker advised him that the gods would be the judge of what was happening at the tomb and the stealing he (Carter) was allowing to happen at the tomb was wrong.

There was much discontent among the workforce, it had never been a happy one and the dialogue between the archaeologists and much of the workforce was never more distant than it was at this time. We knew that Carter had recruited new workers himself, these people had been placed within our fold as communicators, conveying back to the archaeologists details of any dissent they uncovered. Some of the workforce were dismissed by the archaeologists, accused of stealing. This was wrong, most of the Egyptian workers would not steal from the pharaohs, they understood the consequences of doing so, not only would they suffer from the laws of the land but also from the vengeance of the dead. The dismissed workers were merely scapegoats, an effort by the dig team to show the Egyptian governing bodies that they were honest and would not accept any immoral activity at the dig site. It also kept any ill-feeling at bay; workers became reluctant to speak out about anything. Carter maintained an aloofness from workforce issues, leaving his juniors to deal with things like that, yet he would often stop to talk to Egyptians and praise them for their endeavours in supporting the hard work created through the dig. On the day the tomb of Tutankhamun was opened, they discovered fabulous treasures within. At the end of the entrance passageway and to the right was a wall and doorway, standing guard on each side of this were two life-size figures of King Tutankhamun, they had been placed there during the funerary ritual, they faced each other so that between them no one could pass through the doorway they protected, unnoticed. On the forehead of each statue was a depiction of Weret Hekau (the royal cobra). Uraeus, it was claimed, could spit poison and fire at an enemy to protect the king. The goddess Isis used Uraeus to acquire the throne of Egypt for her husband Osiris. Anubis, the jackal dog-headed man, was the son of Osiris and Isis, therefore, despite Carter's belief, links do exist throughout the history of the pharaohs and life and death. The Uraeus set on the brow of the two statues inside the tomb were threatening and menacing in their presence; many Egyptian workers who entered the tomb bowed their heads and dared not look at them. Carter, on inspecting them, touched the effigies and flicked them with his fingers to see what substance they were made from. On doing so it is said he went into a seizure of coughing, this was said to be nothing more than dust contamination.

Later that day, at Carter's house on the edge of the Valley of the Kings, a canary bird he had with him in a cage, as a pet, suffered a ghastly and unusual fate. Carter and a few colleagues, it was said, were dining when a commotion outside his house caused all who heard it to rush out to see from where it emanated. It was the distressed calls of a bird. As they came out, there before them sat a serpent, similar to that in the crown of the sentinels guarding the inner tomb of Tutankhamun, and in its mouth lay the canary; it was dead. It was said by Carter to have died not from any injuries, but the fright of the affair.

The serpent was angered by the delay in devouring its prey and was at once distracted and killed, its head severed from its body. Staff were instructed to clear the mess away, however, they regarded the matter as a warning from the spirit of the dead king against further intrusion into the tomb and were themselves in fear. Carter dismissed it as a natural occurrence and told the staff to get on with the task he had asked of them. He was clearly upset by the incident and angry at his staff for questioning his directions. What is not commonly known is that he later questioned each member of his household staff about why the cage was left insecure and open, thus allowing the serpent access to the bird. He himself examined the cage; it was closed and the door secure. Yet no one had touched it. Carter remained curious how the bird had got out or the serpent in! He believed someone had let the bird out and deliberately brought the serpent to kill it and lost much trust in his staff because of the matter. He demanded complete silence and refused to discuss what had happened with anyone, it was his guests who went on to discuss it with journalists, the Egyptians remained loyal because they were too frightened to utter anything about the underworld. Carter is said to have expressed his worries that someone or something was attempting to frighten him off the site, he believed it was nothing supernatural but of the more physical kind, seeking the rewards of the contents of the tomb.

To cover news of the incident, Carter replaced the canary. A short time later, one of the workers in the Valley was attacked and savaged by a desert dog, it was at night and the dog had been seen watching the various camps where some of the treasures removed from the tomb were first moved to. The superstitious workers claimed that the animal, jet black in colour and thin, lay in the exact pose of the figure of Anubis that had been found within the tomb. The animal sat for hours and was causing some alarm and distress among certain workers. So the worker approached it and tried to move it away. The man was seen walking away with the dog, out of sight behind rocks, at the time there was not a sound of any confrontation or attack taking place. Several hours passed and the man hadn't returned, so several of the group went to look for him. Behind some large rocks they found his dead body, the torso was in a disgusting state, incisions like wounds had been made to the chest and abdomen and his heart had been removed from his internal organs and wasn't to be found anywhere. His face seemed untouched, his eyes were wide open and had the appearance of an insane stare, part of his brain had been pulled down through his nose and lay over his mouth, there were no other marks on his head. The archaeologists were informed of the find and after inspection of the body, were told to bury the man without delay because of the negative publicity such an incident would arouse. The man had no family and his remains were buried under the cover of darkness, there and then in the Valley of the Kings without any formal notification being given to the Egyptian authorities. The dog was never again seen in the area.

Another death occurred through madness when an illiterate worker awoke in the middle of the night screaming in terror, he claimed to have been visited by the boy king, Tutankhamun, who warned him to tell other Egyptian workers who had invaded his tomb and disturbed his peace, not to trust Lord Carnarvon or Howard Carter because they sought fame, wealth and riches that belonged to the Egyptian people, they were sacrificing Egyptian people to the god of the Duat. The man could not be silenced and the madness ensued throughout the night, eventually he was bound to some wooden planks, laid on his back, his head fastened by rope wrapped across the forehead and under the wooden planks to prevent any movement. Finally, after several hours, to the pleasure of his fellow workers he finally fell silent and slept. The following morning when workers checked his condition he was found dead, his tongue had been crudely cut from his mouth and lay by his body, wire had been inserted into and twisted through his lips to seal them closed. Unable to scream or shout, he had suffered an agonising end to his life. Being unable to move he drowned in his blood!

15

The letter by Asim provides some insightful cultural detail into local superstitions that were held by the Egyptian workforce at the time and gives an altogether different, more sinister angle on the history of the curse of King Tutankhamun. It certainly isn't something one might find in a textbook covering the search and excavations to locate and reveal the tomb and its contents.

There exists another mysterious tale, this time involving an infamous psychic healer and occult figure of the twentieth century, Irish-born Count Louis Hamon. As a result of his exceptional skills, he was often bestowed with exotic gifts passed on by grateful clients whom he had helped or cured. According to the legend, the strangest gift of all brought him nothing but trouble. On a visit to Luxor in 1890, Hamon cured a powerful sheik of malaria. To reward him the sheik gave him an unusual gift, the mummified hand of a long-deceased Egyptian princess. The story behind the hand dates back to the time of King Akhenaton, who was in the seventeenth year of his reign of Egypt. Akhenaton quarreled with his daughter over religious matters, and the king did not like her attitude, as she displayed a clear lack of respect for him and his leadership. He ordered priests to disfigure and kill her. This they did and afterwards cut off her right hand and buried it separately and secretly in the Valley of the Kings. The authorities did their best to keep the murder quiet, but her sudden disappearance and the gossip among the courtiers soon revealed what had happened. The death of the princess was viewed with some horror by the people of Egypt, since it was a requirement for the body of the dead to remain intact so that it could enter the afterlife and paradise. Her own father had made sure she could not do this and therefore she was damned for eternity.

Count Hamon's wife disliked the dried-up hand from the first time she saw it, and told her husband to lock it away in an empty wall safe in their London home. In October 1922, Hamon and his wife had reason to reopen the safe – and on doing so, they stood back in terror. There before them was the hand of the murdered princess, but it had altogether changed in its appearance. Mummified for 3,200 years, it had suddenly begun to soften and the flesh was once again growing, looking almost like a healthy hand. The horror of the situation caused Hamon's wife to scream, and she demanded that it must be instantly destroyed. Hamon, by virtue of the fact that he was able to contact the spirits had never before been afraid of anything, but the image of the regrown hand had shocked him. He accepted his wife's request, but told her that he wished to give the hand the best funeral that was possible, since its original owner had been a princess.

On the night of 31 October 1922, Halloween, the burial preparations were complete. The Count later described in a letter to one of his friends, the archaeologist Lord Carnarvon, the format of the burial and how he had laid the hand gently in the fireplace, before reading aloud a passage from the Egyptian Book of the Dead. As he closed the book there was a sudden clap of thunder and the sharp flash of a lightning bolt momentarily illuminated the room, which then fell into total darkness which overcame the entire house. Moments later, the door to the room flew open with a sudden ferocious gust of wind. Hamon's wife fell to the floor in fright, Hamon joined her and together the pair lay there, gripped by the tentacles of ice-cold air. For a few minutes the room was quiet and still. Hamon then raised his eyes to look around and saw, just a few feet from him, the figure of a woman. The apparition was adorned in the royal clothes of ancient Egypt, with the serpent of the Pharaoh's House on her head. Looking more closely he saw that the woman's right arm abruptly ended in a stump. The figure glided across the floor of the room to the roaring fireplace on which the hand had been placed by Hamon. There, it bent forward towards the fire and then, as quickly as it appeared, it was gone. The second it disappeared power was returned to the house and the room once again lit up. A shocked Hamon helped his wife to her feet, but the pair were speechless and still struck by fear. As he looked into the fire he saw that the hand was gone. The couple never saw it again.

Due to the after effects of the ghostly encounter, the Count and his wife were admitted to hospital, where, four days later, Hamon read in the pages of a newspaper that the expedition funded by Lord Carnarvon had discovered the tomb of the ancient pharaoh Tutankhamen, and that they would shortly enter it. Hamon wrote his old friend a letter, pleading with him to think twice before opening the tomb. He wrote: 'I know now that the ancient Egyptians had powers which we do not understand. In the name of our God and father, I ask

17

you not to desecrate that tomb and to take the utmost care if you do.' The rest, as they say, is history! The unnatural deaths in the desert sands of the Valley of the Kings don't end there, as will be seen: they span the globe. However, one further, altogether more infamous death occurred in Egypt, shortly after the tomb was opened...

Chapter 2

Death Has Wings

Off the A34 near Burghclere, north Hampshire, lies Beacon Hill, a place one would hardly associate with ancient Egypt or the curse of the pharaoh's tomb. Yet here, at the top of the hill, lie the mortal remains of the one individual around whom the Western belief in Egyptian curses is based. For this is the final resting place of George Edward Stanhope Molyneux Herbert, 5th Earl of Carnarvon (Lord Carnarvon). From such an elevated position, the grave overlooks the ancestral family seat of Highclere Castle and much of the Hampshire/Berkshire region. I first happened upon the grave by accident back in 1981, when, after climbing the hill with my dog Sam, I saw the black rusty railings that surrounded the grave and wandered over to examine it more closely. To my surprise I read Carnarvon's name on the decaying stone that covered the tomb. It is a wonderfully peaceful, yet powerful location, befitting of a man of his stature who, in death, has possibly become as infamous as King Tutankhamun himself, although unlike King Tutankhamun, Lord Carnarvon will be allowed to rest in peace for eternity. I will always remember the feeling I had when I stood beside Carnarvon's grave alone on that hill: to think that his eyes first gazed upon the wonderful treasures found within the tomb! He smelt and breathed stale Egyptian air that undoubtedly filled the tomb, and he was one of the first to look upon the final remains of a powerful pharaoh. I somehow felt privileged to be there alone with Carnarvon, and again I wondered about his untimely death and all that surrounded it. I tried to envisage his funeral, held at 11am on Saturday 28 April 1923. Immediate family only attended, plus a few loyal household servants. There was no special ceremony for this great man; it was a quiet, peaceful send-off. Beacon Hill was alive with the song

19

of birds. Now, here I was, stood at that very same site, just me and the remains of Lord Carnarvon. It was a special and personal moment for me indeed. I don't believe in coincidence; to me it's little more than an easy way to justify or write off something that is improbable or unlikely. 'Coincidences' are invoked to explain anomalies about Lord Carnarvon's death in Cairo.

Carnarvon had more than a passing interest in Egyptian archaeology for some time before the discovery of King Tutankhamun's tomb. First travelling to Egypt in 1898, he was involved in digs at Thebes in 1905 and later at Dra' Abu El-Naga', where he discovered an 18th Dynasty tomb belonging to a king's son. Teta-Ky was later identified as 'Mayor of the Southern City (Thebes)'. In fact, we also know that he had more than a passing idea about Egyptian curses. Egyptologist Arthur Weigall told of one such instance when mysterious unaccountable happenings occurred.

One of the first discoveries made in the Valley of the Kings was the coffin of a mummified cat, which had been painted black and possessed gleaming, bright yellow eyes. The object was cleaned up and removed to the dig-house. Carnarvon instructed that it be put into his room, but by mistake it was placed in Arthur Weigall's room instead. Returning to the house late at night, Weigall entered his room and bumped into and fell over the coffin, which had been left in the middle of his room. He hurt and bruised his shin. Not long after, the butler in the house was stung by a scorpion and, delirious and in serious pain, he screamed out that he was being pursued by a grey cat. There was nothing Weigall could do to help so he returned to his room and retired to bed. As he was falling asleep he opened his eyes and believed that the mummified cat had turned its head to face him, with a look of anger on its face. The bright yellow eyes were bold and piercing in the darkness of the room. In the distance, Weigall could still hear the insensible cries of the butler. About an hour after he fell asleep, Weigall was awakened by a loud bang – the sound of a gun-shot – which he assumed was a member of the house staff shooting the scorpion. At the same moment, a grey cat leapt over his bed and out of the window. The wooden cat coffin lay in the middle of the floor, now split into two separate pieces, as if whatever was inside had forced it open and released itself from within. Weigall ran to the window and saw the house tabby cat on the garden path. Normally a docile creature, it was hissing and glaring into some nearby bushes, and its back was arched. Shocked by the incident, Weigall spoke to other members of the household staff and explained what had happened and what he saw. The wooden coffin was split in two and there was no sign of any mummified cat. Everyone in the dig-house was of the same opinion: the grey cat that was pursuing the butler and had somehow caused the scorpion to sting, was a malevolent spirit that had caused Weigall to hurt himself when he bumped into its coffin. Carnarvon was in residence at the dig-house when all this occurred, and would have been aware of the idea of the existence of a curse.

By 1907, Carnarvon had been introduced to Howard Carter in Egypt and the pair immediately recognised that a collaboration between them would benefit both sides. They began to excavate new areas and in 1912 a book was published about their work at Thebes: *Five Years' Exploration At Thebes – A Record Of Work Done 1907-1911*. After exhaustive digs across Thebes, often in search of the elusive tomb of King Tutankhamun, in June 1922 Carter suggested one last season of excavations before calling it a day. Carnarvon had all but spent his personal wealth subsidising countless archaeological digs, and this final effort, if it did not find King Tutankhamun's tomb, could have left him in grave financial peril. But Carnarvon believed in Carter, and offered to fund the expedition. The rest, as they say, is history, as the two discovered the boy king's tomb virtually intact.

Two weeks before Carnarvon's death, British novelist Mary Mackay/Corelli wrote a letter that was published in the *New York World* magazine, which seemingly quoted from an obscure book, asserting that, 'dire punishment' would follow intrusion into a sealed tomb.

I cannot but think some risks are run by breaking into the last rest of a king in Egypt whose tomb is specially and solemnly guarded, and robbing him of his possessions. According to a rare book I possess ... 'The Egyptian History of the Pyramids' [an ancient Arabic text], the most dire punishment follows any rash intruder into a sealed tomb. The book ... names secret poisons enclosed in boxes in such wise that those who touch them shall not know how they come to suffer. That is why I ask, was it a mosquito bite that has so seriously infected Lord Carnarvon?

On Thursday 5 April 1923, at around 1.55am, Lord Carnarvon passed away in his room at the Continental Hotel in Cairo. His son, Lord Porchester, 6th Earl of Carnarvon, was present and later remarked to the press that at the precise moment of his father's death all the lights across Cairo went out. Thousands of miles away at Highclere Castle, at exactly the same moment, Carnarvon's three-legged pet dog Susie, howled and died. The curse of the pharaohs was thus brought to the attention of modern society.

It was at this time, aroused by the press speculation about the circumstances attached to Carnarvon's death, that Sir Arthur Conan Doyle revealed his own belief that the pharaoh's curse was potentially the cause of these matters. He suggested that 'elementals' created by Tutankhamun's priests to guard the royal tomb had caused Carnarvon's death. Before long, it was reported that a specific curse had been inscribed in the tomb, a detail that Carter always denied to the outside world. The curse, it was claimed, was written in hieroglyphs adjacent to a winged creature on the door of the second shrine: 'They who enter this sacred tomb shall swift be visited by wings of death.' The exact phraseology has varied with the passage of time, dependent upon the imagination of the writer. In an attempt to ridicule and dismiss such reports, the authorities revealed that Lord Carnarvon's death had not been suspicious or sinister. He had cut into a mosquito bite while shaving, which had become infected. Carnarvon was already weak through exhaustion from over-exertion in Egypt, and he contracted pneumonia and shortly after passed away. The official reports on the cause of death, however, did little or nothing to dispel the belief that the curse was responsible, since mosquitoes have wings and the curse reportedly included the phrase 'wings of death.'

Carter dismissed any suggestion of a curse and denied the existence of any curse in the tomb. However, local people who worked on the dig site claimed that two curses were inscribed at different points of access into the tomb and its inner confines. A local Egyptologist, Abdul Aziz, explained in 2008:

The mystery remains why no one took any notice of local people involved in the excavations. Carter and Carnarvon did their utmost to shut down communication within the Valley of the Kings. They wanted no word or secrets revealed to the outside world and if you look at some of the statements ascribed to both Carnarvon and Carter, they were struggling to cope with the amount of worldwide interest ranging from visiting dignitaries to the press, all wanting to see something of note or to get a story. It remains unofficial but most dignitaries gained access to the tomb by negotiating an access fee, for this they could be given a tour by Howard Carter and receive an irrelevant artifact as a souvenir, not always from the tomb! Both Carnarvon and Carter worked hard to stop information leaking out to the press or elsewhere. A financial deal had been prearranged with The Times newspaper as sole reporting body for the excavation. It was the local Egyptians who worked on the site that knew the truth about what was happening in the Valley of the Kings. Within countless different families there exist stories of unaccountable things that occurred during the dig for King Tutankhamun's tomb. It isn't about mass hysteria, or tales that are created to earn them some attention, most of the families don't and won't repeat them because they live in fear that if they discuss the dead and the underworld then they will suffer too. This fear is something that is tangible, it's clear when one speaks with them that they do not like or wish to be associated with it.

It was common knowledge that both Carnarvon and Carter would deliberately spread propaganda among the workers, denying the existence of Egyptian magic and spiritual matters, such as the perils of the underworld. This propaganda served a dual purpose: it helped keep the workers' minds on the tasks they were set, dispelling tales of the dead and of vendettas of long since dead pharaohs' priests, and secondly, any loose tongues among the work force would have little or nothing of any mystical note to convey to an inquiring press. Such detail comes from many different sources, not just one family. Likewise, Howard Carter's dislike, some say it was fear, of the black desert dogs or jackals. He admitted seeing these creatures running wild in the deserts of Egypt after the discovery of King Tutankhamun's tomb; his servants claimed he was terrified by them and believed them to be evil and real life portrayals of Anubis. There are many tales of mysterious deaths and incidents surrounding many tombs in the Valley of the Kings, but it is King Tutankhamun that resonates most loudly with the public.

When one looks at the some of the things that happened when Carnarvon passed away, it doesn't add up. For instance, the lights going out across Cairo at exactly the same time he expired. I know it has been counterclaimed by some so called 'authorities' that this was a common occurrence, well, it wasn't that common. It wasn't reliable but it certainly wasn't something that happened with any frequency, this is just another way for the authorities to dismiss suggestions that some unexplainable phenomenon may have occurred, which helped supplement the propaganda that Egypt was curse-free. Local Egyptians thought Carter, Carnarvon and others associated with the excavations to be foolish for ignoring the dangers and the warnings of the gods of the underworld. It is well known that a curse or curses were found inscribed on the tomb of King Tutankhamun. Five different and unconnected families speak of how their fore-fathers working there were instructed by Carter to break up and destroy, then bury, a stone plinth upon which a curse had been carved. Carter had already taken a hammer to the object, smashing it into several pieces so it was unreadable. He instructed the men to smash it into tiny particles and then go forth and bury it in the desert sand at individual points so that it could never again be found, or reassembled! When asked what the object was, he angrily exclaimed that it was nothing to do with a curse, but rather, something that was unhealthy and carried the threat of disease to everyone. The men asked him why he wanted this carried out during the hours of darkness? Carter told them that he felt there would be least disruption during that time and the fewer the number of people who knew about it, the better it would be *for everyone. Each of the workers who carried out this task was paid by Carter and all were told not to discuss the matter with anyone else. Later, a group of workers overheard Carter discussing the plinth and the curse inscribed upon it with Carnarvon. The two men were in a tent and believed no one was listening. Carter had told Carnarvon that it (the curse and the plinth) must never be mentioned or discussed by them or anyone else again; he said it would strike fear into the workforce and the excavations might be stopped. Carter, especially, spent the rest of his life denying the existence of a curse. However, what many people do not realise is that shortly before his death on 2 March 1939, Carter was haunted by images in his mind, images of Anubis.*

(This in fact is a detail I have previously been told, that Carter didn't die quietly of heart failure at his Collingham Gardens home in Kensington, London. Instead he was tormented and suffered night terrors, with visions of Anubis sitting on his chest, staring down at him). Nowhere will you find such detail recorded in any official document. Science and social pressures do not allow a man as influential as Howard Carter in his own discipline to suddenly proclaim a belief in something so institutionally unacceptable as a pharaoh's curse. I say 'institutionally unacceptable', because it is not the masses who distinguish reality from fiction, it is the Establishment that does so. Any suggestion that Carter had altered his beliefs before his death would undermine the status quo and therefore damage the very infrastructure upon which society is based. Curses, therefore, simply cannot exist because the Establishment dismisses them as nonsense.

It's interesting to note that an inscription was found inside the tomb by Carter, on a statue of Anubis, which read: 'It is I who hinder the sand from choking the secret chamber. I am for the protection of the deceased.' Perhaps this stuck with Carter, causing him to consider Anubis such a danger to him as he neared death? If this was the end of the curse material associated with King Tutankhamun then it would be reasonable to assume that Lord Carnarvon's demise was not suspicious, and nor were the deaths of workers in the Valley of the

Kings. Sadly, the deaths and curious incidents don't end there; after the death of Lord Carnarvon they increased in quantity and intrigue. From the long list of incidents and deaths that were suspicious in their very nature, here we will mention just a few.

Sir Bruce Ingham was given a gift by Howard Carter, a paperweight which contained a tiny mummified hand. Around the wrist of this limb was a scarab bracelet. The following inscription had been added to the object: 'Cursed be he who moves my body, I'm sure and severs my hand and uses it as a trinket.' Alternatively, according to some reports, it read: 'Cursed be he who moves my body. To him shall come fire, water and pestilence'. Not long after accepting the gift, Ingham's house burned to the ground and later, as it was being rebuilt, the land was flooded. It is said that Ingham believed the cursed paperweight was to blame for the ill fortune. The wording of the alternative curse appears to have been adapted to fit the scenario that befell Ingham, fire and flood.

The story surrounding Prince Ali Kamel Fahmi Bey, a 23-year-old Egyptian who, it is claimed, had visited the tomb of King Tutankhamun and been handed a personal gift (artifact), has a more final end. Fahmi Bey was, in the early hours of 11 July 1923, shot dead by his wife, Marie-Marguerite, in the Savoy Hotel, London. Ali Kamel Fahmi Bey was not actually a prince, but did little to counter suggestions that he was. According to his murderous wife of six months, he was violent and had temper tantrums if he did not get his own way. Being Egyptian, and more since his visit to the Valley of the Kings, he had talked openly of the curse of the pharaohs and believed that the gift he had accepted had associated him with the desecration of the tomb, making him likely to suffer. His belief wasn't too much of an exaggeration, since not only was he murdered, but his integrity also suffered and his reputation was all but destroyed in the subsequent trial of his killer, who walked free from court after being acquitted. Marie-Marguerite moved to Paris where, as a result of her acquittal, she became a minor celebrity, even appearing in minor roles in the occasional French film. One such performance saw her playing an Egyptian wife! Perhaps feeling somewhat invincible, she almost immediately made a claim against the estate of her late husband. Not only did she think she would get away with killing a man, but she also then wanted access to his fortune! Her attempt failed as Fahmi had made no will. Undeterred, and keen to get her hands on the wealth, the sinister side of Marie-Marguerite began to emerged. She came up with a ludicrous tale, pretendeding that she had been pregnant by Fahmi, and had subsequently borne a son (the child being entitled to his father's fortune). The allegation was easily disproved. She was socially ostracised as a result, and eventually became something of a laughing stock in Parisian society. She never remarried and rarely discussed the case or her past again. She died on 2 January 1971 in Paris.

George Jay Gould was a wealthy financier who subsidised some of the work at the tomb. When he visited Egypt and the tomb in May 1923 he fell ill, dying of pneumonia on the French Riviera on 16 May 1923, as a result of the illness contracted in Egypt. He was fifty-nine. Prior to his death, Gould, it was alleged, said he could see and hear the spirits of the pharaohs surrounding him, with the mighty jackal-headed god (Anubis) drawing the last breath out of him. Then we have Lord Carnarvon's half-brother, Aubrey Herbert; this unfortunate man went blind. It was claimed that rotting teeth had somehow interfered with his vision. In an attempt to regain his sight, he had every single tooth pulled from his head, to no avail; he never regained his sight. However, he died of blood poisoning as a result of the surgery, on 26 September 1923, just five months after the death of his half-brother Lord Carnarvon! Hugh Gerard Evelyn-White, an eminent scholar, was so afraid of the curse that he killed himself before the terrors of Tutankhamun could harm him at his home at 33 Victoria Terrace, Leeds on 9 September 1924. Evelyn-White was a respected archaeologist who had helped in the excavations of the tomb, and after witnessing the deaths within the Valley of the Kings, and later those of some of his fellows associated with the dig, he took his own life by hanging himself. He left a suicide note: 'I have succumbed to a curse which forces me to disappear.' Here was a man in good health, just fifty years of age and at the peak of his career. He had no known reason to commit suicide and among those who knew him he was regarded as content. Yet he was clearly haunted by demons, hence his tragic death and sinister-sounding suicide note.

Georges Aaron Bénédite was a French Egyptologist and curator at the Louvre. Bénédite is noted for his discovery of the tomb of Akhethetep at Saqqara on 28 March 1903. In March 1926 he visited the tomb of King Tutankhamun and shortly afterwards died in Luxor. He had appeared to be well and in good spirits before he entered the tomb, but was struck down by sudden illness after leaving. One of America's leading Egyptologists, scholar Professor Aaron Ember, a good friend of Carnarvon who had received artifacts from the tomb, died in 1926 when his house burned down. The following is the report of what happened to Ember, published by the American Oriental Society in 1926:

Dr. Aaron Ember, Professor of Egyptology at Johns Hopkins University, lost his life in a terrible tragedy which occurred at his residence at Windsor Hill, Baltimore, Md., in the early morning of 31 May. He and Mrs. Ember had been entertaining friends until a late hour, and must have gone to sleep after retiring. Apparently less than an hour after the guests had departed, a chance passer-by noticed smoke pouring from the house, and attempted without success to arouse the family. Just what happened in that house after the inmates did awaken will never be known. Mrs. Ember, attempting to save her invalid six-year old son, was overcome and burned to death with her child before aid could reach her, and a similar fate overtook the maid. Professor Ember, fearfully burned, managed to reach the roof of the side porch, and was helped to the ground, where he was with difficulty restrained from rushing into the blazing house again in search of his wife and child. Fire engines which had been summoned arrived too late to save the lives of those left in the house. Professor Ember was hurried to hospital where he died of his burns the following day. In the brief intervals in which he was fully conscious he could give very little account of the tragedy except that the family awoke to find the house in flames, and that Mrs. Ember told him to rescue the manuscript of the book he was writing while she saved Robert.

The manuscript upon which Ember had been working was apparently entitled: *The Egyptian Book of the Dead.* It is said that privately Ember was a firm believer in the curse of the pharaohs. Ember was in fact credited by Egyptologists with having definitively established, for the first time, the common origin of the Egyptian and Israelite tongues. Physicians at the West Baltimore General Hospital where he died said that when Ember was told of the loss of his family and the manuscript, he gave up the will to live. A few days later, the Mayor of Baltimore, Howard W. Jackson, after an investigation, exonerated firemen of charges of tardiness in reaching the fire.

Richard Bethell was Howard Carter's secretary and the first person after Howard Carter to set foot inside the tomb of King Tutankhamun. Bethell died on 15 November 1929, having been found in his bed at Mayfair's exclusive Bath Club. It was claimed that prior to his sudden death, he had been a healthy man and that he had died of a coronary thrombosis. Despite the assertions of others, there is no evidence whatsoever to support the allegation that he was suffocated with a pillow. His father, Lord Westbury, committed suicide in London on 21 February 1930. It was reported in the press that 'mortal fear of the curse of the pharaohs against all who disturb their eternal rest' drove him to his death. The elderly Lord leapt from a window of his seventh floor flat in St James' Court. He left behind in his room a black-edged note stating: 'I really cannot stand any more horrors'. Also found in his room were countless exquisite relics of Egypt. A further sinister occurrence is attached to this death, as on 25 February 1930, as Lord Westbury's funeral cortège moved through London towards the crematorium at Golders Green, the hearse containing the Lord's body knocked down and killed eight-year-old Joseph Greer in a street close to the child's Battersea home. There were several vehicles in the cortège, yet it was the hearse containing the body of an alleged victim of the curse that struck and killed the poor boy.

Another to die was radiologist Archibald Douglas Reid: he had X-rayed the body of King Tutankhamun before it was moved to the museum of Cairo. The day after he carried out this task he fell sick and was sent back to England. It was said he exhibited signs of exhaustion – which he strongly refuted – but he died three days later on 17 January 1924. Not long after Carnarvon's demise, another archaeologist, Arthur Cruttenden Mace, a leading member of the expedition, fell into a coma at the Hotel Continental after complaining of tiredness. It has been claimed that he exhibited symptoms of arsenic poisoning. Mace was forced to retire from Egyptian archaeological work and returned to London where he died in 1928. His illness was said to have left the expedition medical expert and local doctors baffled.

In the years that followed, deaths and incidents continued. Mohammed Ibrahim, Egypt's Director of Antiquities, opposed the release of treasures from the tomb so that they could be exhibited in Paris in 1966. It was Ibrahim's responsibility to sign the contract releasing the artifacts, but he did not want to do so. It is known that Ibrahim pleaded with the Egyptian authorities to keep the relics in Cairo. One of his reasons for the request was that for many months he had suffered terrifying nightmares of a painful and agonising death should he allow them to leave the country. In one last effort to prevent the release of the items, a desperate Ibrahim admitted he believed that ill fortune would befall many if the artifacts left their home in Egypt. The authorities dismissed this as nonsense. A distraught Ibrahim left that final meeting with the government officials and, according to several eyewitnesses, he stepped out into a clear road. There was no visible traffic and no sound of any vehicle approaching; it was a bright, clear sunny day. Within moments, the sound of a car was heard and bystanders saw Ibrahim struck down by a vehicle that killed him instantly. His death was attributed to him being emotionally distraught and not concentrating on the road, but witnesses claim otherwise.

In 1969 Richard Adamson, said to be the last surviving member of the original 1923 expedition, left an interesting testimony. Adamson was vocally dismissive of the talk of any curse and often enjoyed the limelight, talking to the press about how he had guarded the tomb of King Tutankhamun and nothing strange ever happened. It is said that on one occasion he spoke out against the curse, and within 24 hours his wife died. Later, after he again talked of the matter, his son suffered a broken back in an aircraft crash. Eventually, after another public outburst in defiance against the curse in an interview on British television, he left the television studios and called a taxi. During that journey the taxi was involved in an accident. Adamson was thrown from the vehicle when it crashed, and an oncoming lorry managed to swerve to avoid hitting Adamson, apparently missing his head by a few inches. Adamson was taken to hospital suffering from fractures and bruises. It was then that he was forced to admit: 'Until now I refused to believe that my family's misfortunes had anything to do with the curse. But now I am not so sure.'

Dr Gamal Mehrez, Ibrahim's successor in Cairo as Egypt's Director of Antiquities, died on 4 February 1972. Unlike his predecessor, he scoffed at and poured scorn on the legend of a curse; he often stated that his entire life had been spent working in Egyptology and that the deaths and misfortune associated with the curse were 'pure coincidence'. He died of a brain haemorrhage while experts packed priceless Egyptian relics into an RAF plane for transport to England. Tragedy then struck the crew members of the aircraft. When Flight Lieutenant Rick Laurie died of a heart attack in 1976, his wife is said to have declared: 'It's the curse of Tutankhamun – the curse has killed him.' A friend of the family said that Rick Laurie had been haunted by worry that he carried the curse and feared for his life. He had been a fit and healthy man, and his heart attack came out of the blue and shocked everyone. Another serviceman, flight engineer Ken Parkinson, suffered a heart attack every year, at the same time as the flight aboard the Britannia aircraft which brought the treasures to England, until a final fatal attack killed him in 1978. It should be noted that before the Tutankhamun mission, both of these service personnel had undergone medicals and been pronounced fit by military doctors. A somewhat more apocryphal tale relating to the same flight concerns the Chief Technical Officer, Ian Lansdown, who is said to have kicked the crate that contained the death mask of the boy king. 'I've just kicked the most expensive thing in the world,' he is said to have quipped. On disembarking from the aircraft a ladder he was using mysteriously broke, and in the fall he broke the leg with which he had kicked the crate. Flight Lieutenant Jim Webb, who was also aboard the aircraft, lost everything he owned after a fire devastated his home. One of the stewards, Brian Rounsfall, is said to have admitted playing cards on the crate containing artifacts, generally thought to be the crate housing the death mask or sarcophagus, during the flight to England. He later suffered two heart attacks. Finally, a woman officer on board the plane later had to leave the RAF after undergoing a serious medical operation.

I contacted the RAF to make formal enquiries about the stories relating to the plane crew. Perhaps understandably, the response was 'no comment'. Are all these incidents – and there are many more that can be associated with them – merely coincidences, as the Establishment would prefer us to believe? Or could there really be some unnatural force at work? Skeptics virtually always use Howard Carter as an example in dismissing the curse of King Tutankhamun. Carter lived on for many years after Carnarvon and others were seemingly struck down. Yet we now know that Carter, despite claims to the contrary, did suffer nightmares and terrors relating to Anubis, and it is further claimed that he physically saw several Anubis-like black desert dogs in the Egyptian sands during later archaeological work. To this day black dogs are still viewed as spectral dogs, devil dogs or hell hounds, and in some religions they are believed to be the devil masquerading in animal form. As we know, ancient Egyptians believed the black dog or jackal, Anubis, was the patron of mummification and guardian of the path through the underworld. Prayers to the god Anubis can be found carved in most ancient Egyptian tombs. Anubis is generally portrayed as a man with the head of a dog/jackal; the head is black and represents his position as god of the dead. None of this was alien to Carter or Carnarvon, yet both, particularly in the latter stages of their lives, spoke of seeing and apparently fearing an encounter with Anubis.

Chapter 3

The Curse of the London Mummy

The curse of the mummy is undoubtedly the most popular and gripping tale emanating from Egypt, and it has existed for well over a century. In 1821 an exhibition opened in London's Piccadilly at a property built in 1812 and known as the Egyptian Hall, a private museum of natural history. The exhibition opened on 1 May 1821 and was unique, the first of its sort in Europe: a reconstruction of an Egyptian pharaoh's tomb originally discovered in 1818 by former circus strongman and later Egyptian excavator, Giovanni Belzoni. Before a crowd of hundreds, Belzoni appeared wrapped entirely from head to foot in bandages. Some 2,000 visitors flocked to the exhibition on its opening day, most amazed by the artifacts (some authentic, some created) that were on display, including two genuine mummies.

In August 1821, a new artifact was added to the display. It was a white alabaster sarcophagus, measuring ten feet in length and bearing ornate inscriptions and hieroglyphs. The sarcophagus was translucent when lit from behind, enhancing the remarkable inscriptions. On the base of the coffin, where the pharaoh's body would lie, was a full-length depiction of a goddess (later found to be the goddess Mut). This was no ordinary find, and it was later discovered that the sarcophagus belonged to none other than 19th Dynasty ruler Sethos (Seti I). Seti I had succeeded his father Ramesses I in 1291 BC, and in turn was succeeded in 1278 BC by his own son, Ramesses II, Egypt's most famous ruler, commonly referred to as 'Ramesses the Great'. The inscription on the side of the object portrayed Seti's journey to the underworld – *The Book of the Gates*, which is discussed elsewhere. It is worth noting that there was no sinister undertone or mention of supernatural curses attached or associated with the exhibition, a clear indication that such matters were introduced or recognised at a much later date.

It was not until 1894 that a denouncer of Egypt's corrupt and backward ways, Sir Arthur Conan Doyle, created a fictional mummy exacting the revenge of a Victorian black magician in his short story 'Lot No. 249', first published in *Harper's*. Thereafter, a veritable library of authors repeated, enhanced and added various supernatural twists to the tale.

In 1932, legendary actor Boris Karloff played the first ever on-screen mummy, becoming the revived Egyptian priest Imhotep in the now classic film *The Mummy*. In more recent times, during the filming of television series *Downton Abbey* at Highclere Castle, the ancestral home of the Carnarvon family, it was claimed by actress Shirley MacLaine, a woman who believes in reincarnation and thinks that her pet dog Terry (a rat terrier) is a reincarnation of Anubis, saw ghostly figures and pictures inexplicably fall from the walls of the castle during filming of the show. MacLaine believed these were spirits associated with Egyptian King Tutankhamun. She inaccurately stated: 'They had the tomb of King Tut in the basement'.

Thus we come to the story of exhibit BM22542 – the unique reference number given to the inner coffin lid (more commonly referred to as the mummy board) by the British Museum. The British Museum has been open to the public since 15 January 1759, although it was established in 1753. Today it has over seven million artifacts on display. The exhibit to which we refer was originally donated to the museum on behalf of Mr Arthur Wheeler by Mrs Warwick Hunt, of Holland Park, London, in July 1889. Its provenance has never truly been established, but it is perhaps one of the most infamous and written about artifacts on display in the Egyptian Room. It is widely believed across the world to be the mummy board of the priestess of Amen-Ra, said to have lived some 1,500 years before Christ. The board itself measures roughly 5 feet 4 inches in length. On her death, the remains of the priestess were mummified and placed in an ornate wooden coffin that was buried deep within a vault in Luxor, Egypt, just off the banks of the River Nile.

To gain a greater understanding of the curse that is said to be associated with the object, we must first identify Amen-Ra. Records show that Amen was one of the gods who was well known to Egyptians in very early times: his name can be found within the pyramid texts. The name 'Amen' means 'that which cannot be seen' or 'hidden'. In the hymns to Amen, his name can also be translated to mean: 'hidden to his children', or 'hidden to gods and men'. As a Thebes deity he was regarded as the god of the wind before becoming known as the chief of gods. He is often considered to be the king of gods. It is said that the term 'hidden' refers to the setting sun at the end of the day, becoming hidden to mortals. As was often the case in Egyptian religion, the gods were often combined with other deities, to satisfy as many worshippers as possible. Amen's absolute power came from him being combined with the sun god Ra. Ra was acknowledged to be the father of all living things, the physical father. If you look more closely at the use of the term Ra when associated with Amen, you can see that Amen was the god who could not be seen by mortal eyes, and the attributes applied to him were eternal – he was a powerful god. Controversially, some suggest that the word 'Amen', said after Christian prayer, refers to this god, and that the Vatican Church, wishing to pay tribute to him, documented his life and transformed it into their own history of religion, calling it the Bible, with Jesus Christ as the central figure. It is claimed that the life of Jesus was based on that of Ra, who existed some 3,000 years earlier. However, in this discussion our focus is on the mummy board and not the foundation of religion, though Amen-Ra was without doubt a highly respected god.

The board itself is decorated with the painted face of a woman. It is described by the eminent Egyptologist E.A. Wallis Budge, in his work *The Mummy: A Handbook of Egyptian Funerary Archaeology*, as being 'decorated with an elaborate pectotal, figures of the gods, sacred symbols of Osiris and Isis, and at the foot, between crowned uraei, is a cartouche containing the prenomen and nomen of Amenhetep I, Tcheserkara Amenhetep, one of the earliest kings of the XVIII dynasty, and a great benefactor of the priesthood of Amen at Thebes'. The story of how the board arrived in Britain is important, since much has been made of this and it forms the infrastructure of the curse itself.

An Oxford graduate, published author, horse breeder, society gentleman and amateur archaeologist and friend of the rival Egyptologists Ernest Wallis Budge and William Flinders Petrie, named Thomas Douglas Murray (1841–1911), was one of a group of four wealthy young Englishmen who had been visiting excavation sites at Luxor since 1866. In 1899 the group, who were in Luxor, were offered and invited to buy an exquisite mummy case that was said to contain the remains of a princess of Amen-Ra. Having examined it, each of the group wanted to independently own the object. Each argued his case and gave reasons why it should be his, but no argument was persuasive enough to win the board. The group decided to draw lots to determine who would buy and own it. The man who won (some claim it was Murray, but the story suggests it could not have been) paid several thousand pounds and had the coffin removed to his hotel. Mysterious noises and moaning were heard coming from his room; strange wailing voices that sounded almost hypnotic in tone. A few hours later, the man, who was now seemed preoccupied by his own thoughts, was seen leaving the hotel alone, and later walking out towards the desert. He never returned to the hotel and was never seem again. The following day, Murray was out shooting when he slipped and inadvertently shot himself in the arm. He needed urgent medical attention, so the group tried to get from Thebes to Cairo as quickly as possible. They sailed the Nile, but strong headwinds prevented them from making a swift journey and it was ten days before Murray could get any medical treatment. By that time, gangrene had set in and Murray's arm had to be amputated. The third man in the foursome found on his return home that his family's fortune had been lost. Meanwhile, the fourth man was struck down by a severe illness, lost his job and was seemingly reduced to selling matches in the street. It was a harrowing tale indeed, and one that was sufficient to convince much of the British population that a curse did exist.

When the mummy board eventually arrived in London, its owner, who believed it to house a malevolent spirit from another world, attempted to exorcise the object and house. A well-known authority on the occult, Madame Helena Blavatsky, was requested to visit the premises. Within moments of arriving at the house, Blavatsky gripped her chest and was forced to sit down as she was seized with a shivering fit. She could sense the evil within and she wandered through every room in the house in an attempt to locate the source. In the attic she found the mummy board and identified it as the home of the evil entity. In terror, the owner asked her to carry out an exorcism, to which Blavatsky retorted: 'There is no such thing as exorcism. Evil remains evil forever. Nothing can be done about it. I implore you to get rid of this evil as soon as possible'.

This tale of the visit of Madame Blavatsky is extraordinary, as she died from influenza in 1891, which casts doubt on other elements of the story. There is however, a further twist that can be revealed here for the very first time. An English medium was involved in the episode. This was Robert James Lees, who was a Leicester born, London-based spiritualist medium and a firm believer in reincarnation. In private communications he stated that he believed in the curse of the Egyptian pharaohs, and had once visited a certain well-known London home in Portland Place and been asked to purge a malevolent Egyptian spirit that resided in a coffin-like artifact stored there. He had neither the power nor authority to do this, so advised the owner to be rid of the casket with all haste! Whether it was the mummy board of Amen-Ra or another artifact is not known. Lees, despite being accused of being a fantasist, has never once been accused of fraud, unusual in skeptical Victorian society, where mediums were often viewed as illicit moneymaking fraudsters. Lees was outspoken in his beliefs and infamously claimed to know the identity of Victorian London's Jack the Ripper: a well-known physician and private surgeon to none other than HM Queen Victoria. As questionable as such a claim seems, some documentary evidence can support his belief.

When the mummy board arrived at the British Museum, many lives had been lost and permanently damaged since it became the property of Western owners, yet the anguish and carnage did not end there. In late 1906, Will Scott, a Scottish (Borders-based) writer and storyteller, carried out his own research into the phenomenon. Scott had relatives who had visited Egypt and told him many tales of cursed Egyptian tombs, stolen artifacts and of the pain, suffering and mayhem such curses could cause. In private letters, Scott was able to physically identify at least seven people who had died as a result of the so-called cursed coffin lid. Robert Batty told him:

When we moved the thing (coffin lid) into its place of storage at the British Museum, it was taken to a room where it could be prepared for display. Inside its crate no one felt it to be of any danger, and the carter who was crushed by the wagon transporting it to the museum was said to have tripped and fallen into the path of the reversing wagon. At the time, no one believed it to be part of any curse, it was just one of those things, an accident. It was only when people rushed to help him that they found him not to be screaming in pain, but in fear! He claimed that he felt a gust of wind, followed by what he thought was a strangely dressed woman floating close to the back of the wagon, he described her as ghost like and having long dark hair and a very angry face. He could hear hissing serpents and then saw a black dog-like creature looking down at him from the back of the wagon. Within moments, the ghostly women had seized him by both arms, her grip was strong, she blew cold air into his face and mouth that caused him to gasp until it filled his lungs with what felt like a blast of ice, thus preventing him from crying out, she then pulled him down into the path of the reversing wagon.

The man was quickly removed to hospital and the coffin lid taken inside. It was then that others present claimed to hear strange whispering voices coming from the shadows. One person, a Welshman called Davies, thought he saw two snakes slithering on the floor; other people, including me, heard a woman's scream, it was a shrill terrifying noise much as a banshee would sound I would imagine. Many of those present went into faints as a sickly death-like smell filled the air, it was a sweet smell, but deathly. When I saw the face that was painted on the lid I felt every hair stand up on my body, it was like looking death in the face, it looked tortured. We were each given a sum of money not to discuss anything with anyone outside the museum, we were told that the curse was evil and to talk about it may invoke the curse on each of us. It's only now that I feel safe and able to freely mention it to you. I know two fellows who died within days of handling that thing, fit and healthy men. One just dropped to the floor dead, there was no warning and no illness, the other was in his bed and had woken his wife with his tormented screaming. Asking him what was wrong, he said he had seen a tall man whispering over him, then there was a weight on his body, it was a black dog that sat on his chest, snarling at him. No sooner had he told his wife about this dream, that he felt pain in his chest, like someone was pulling his heart from his body, within a few moments, he was dead.

Will Scott also claimed that other people visiting the museum had witnessed a snarling and ferocious large black dog wandering the corridors, and that the authorities were doing their utmost to stifle such speculation and claims. The interest in the mummy lid had become almost frenzied, and everyone wanted to know more about the cursed object and the evil presence attached to it. Gradually the story became so popular that many eminent figures of the time opted to get involved and publish their own opinion on the matter.

Also in 1906, a close friend of Sir Arthur Conan Doyle, Bertram Fletcher Robinson, once editor of the *Daily Express*, carried out twelve weeks of personal research at the museum. His aim was to disprove the tales surrounding the mummy case. It is claimed that on 21 January 1907 he died suddenly at his London home. Conan Doyle was interviewed about his friend's death and said:

It is impossible to say with absolute certainty if this is true. If we had proper occult powers we could determine it, but I warned Fletcher Robinson against concerning himself with the mummy at the British Museum ... I told him he was tempting fate by pursuing his enquiries, but he was fascinated and would not desist. Then he was overtaken by illness. The immediate cause of his death was typhoid fever, but that is the way the elementals guarding the mummy might act. They could have guided Mr Robinson into a series of such circumstances as would lead him to contract the disease, and thus cause his death – just as in Lord Carnarvon's case, human illness was the primary cause of death.

There is much more intrigue to reveal. In 2003, it was suggested by researcher and author Roger Garrick-Steele, that Robinson was in fact the sole author of *The Hound of the Baskervilles*, and that Conan Doyle had plagiarised the work, and that Conan Doyle was allegedly having an affair with Fletcher Robinson's wife (Gladys). According to Garrick-Steele, Conan Doyle persuaded the wife to administer laudanum to her husband to kill him, which she did. If this assertion seems far-fetched, then the following detail will cause more than a few brows to furrow.

Conan Doyle was a member of a group called the Spiritualists. This group believed that the spirits of the dead have both the ability and the inclination to communicate with the living. Spiritualism was popular at the time, with perhaps nine million believers worldwide. As a result of his beliefs, Conan Doyle would often debate with skeptics, arguing the case for the existence of life after death. One such skeptic was legendary escape artist Harry Houdini. Houdini made it a personal crusade to expose Spiritualism as fakery committed only by charlatans, denouncing the mediums who were well paid to speak with the dead. He successfully unveiled many fraudsters before he died of peritonitis on 31 October (Halloween!) in 1926. In 2007, Houdini's great-nephew George Hardeen said that no autopsy was carried out on Houdini, and that he believes that the death was deliberately caused by a group called the Spiritualists. Matters take a more suspicious turn when one examines the contents of a letter sent by Conan Doyle to a fellow spiritualist. Discussing the American showman, he said Houdini 'would get his just deserts very exactly meted out... I think there is a general pay day coming soon'. Speculation on what he meant by this is for another time and another book, but the plot thickens…

A photographer who took images of the coffin lid developed the plates himself. When he viewed them, instead of seeing the painted female face on the lid, he saw that of a malevolent woman of Egyptian origin. He was so horrified and tortured by the images, that without further ado he returned to his home, locked himself in a bedroom and shot himself through the head, leaving a suicide note declaring that he was possessed by an ancient spirit that urged him to commit sinful acts. A school teacher, visiting the museum to inspect the lid, ridiculed stories of a curse being associated with it. She fell on leaving the building broke one of her arms. A short time later, the daughter of the Marchioness of Salisbury visited the museum to see the lid. She mocked and spoke rudely of the pictured face on the mummy board. Within moments, and before she left the museum, she fell on some stairs and sprained an ankle.

Eventually the mummy board of Amen-Ra was installed in the Egyptian Room at the museum, and the problems associated with it continued. Eric Simms told me of a tale which had existed in his family for as long as he could recall. A family relative was a paid night watchman who was frequently on duty at the museum. Within a few days of the mummy board being placed on display eerie happenings began to occur. The first report of strange goings-on was when some of the men heard a woman crying and wailing. They traced the sound to the mummy board. When they stood beside it the crying ceased, changing to what was described as a ghoulish cackling and whispering in a foreign language. The matter was reported to the management but dismissed as foolish trickery played upon the men by other watchmen. Over a brief period of time the unexplainable occurrences got worse, as other exhibits in the room were hurled about and damaged. Matters came to a head when one night watchman, who appeared to suffer more from the actions of the entity than others, died of fright one evening while on duty. The authorities dismissed the death as a heart attack, but the dead man was apparently fit and healthy and had never previously suffered serious illness. Several other watchmen left their positions, seemingly through fear. Lower grade museum staff were terrified of the curse and cleaners refused to go near the mummy board. On one occasion, a visitor, dubious about any suggestion that an old piece of wood could cause such chaos, stood above the object and flicked a cloth at the face painted on the board, laughing out loud as he did so and demanding that the entity reveal itself or cause him harm. Nothing happened and he scoffed at the mention of a curse. He left the museum unharmed and returned to his home, but his child died of measles soon afterwards. The adverse publicity meant that the museum authorities had the mummy board removed and taken down to the basement for temporary storage. Within a few days, one of the porters who had carried the board was hospitalised when he fell ill. Shortly afterwards, the supervisor of the move was found dead as he sat at his desk. Again it was announced that his death was due to natural causes.

There have been claims that the mummy board was accountable for thousands of deaths, including the sinking of the *Titanic*! There is no evidence for this at all, and I mention it here simply to give the reader an overview of how the story of the mummy board of Amen-Ra has evolved and changed. In the retelling it is said that an American archaeologist paid a good price for the mummy board and arranged for its removal to his home in New York. So in April 1912 the new owner transported his acquisition on the new White Star liner making its maiden voyage to New York. Examination of the inventory logs of the *Titanic* reveals that no mummy board, mummy or other such artifact was on board, so this part of the story can be safely disregarded.

Sir Ernest Wallis Budge, the Keeper of Egyptian and Assyrian Antiquities at the British Museum, added his own fuel to the flames surrounding the curse. Budge, who was well respected and had translated the Egyptian *Book of the Dead*, was quoted as saying, 'Never print what I saw in my lifetime, but the mummy case of Princess Amen-Ra caused the war'. In 1934, however, Wallis Budge issued an altogether different 'official' statement, claiming that the British Museum had never possessed a mummy, a coffin or cover that had been involved in any unusual events. He confirmed the case had never been sold since it arrived at the museum, and that it had never been on the *Titanic*. In fact, it had never left the museum at any point since its arrival (aside from a brief period when it was stored in the basement during the First World War). Wallis Budge died in the same year he made this declaration. Was he too struck down by the malevolent curse for daring to dismiss it? I will leave the reader to decide, with a full reproduction of a an article published in the *New York Times* in 1923.

WEIRD MISFORTUNES BLAMED ON MUMMY
Saturday 7 April 1923 Beautiful but Malignant Priestess Is Said to Resent Touching Her Coffin Lid
IT IS IN BRITISH MUSEUM
Officials Call Stories Myths, but Superstitious Even Blame Her for Sinking of Titanic
The New York Times Company

Special Cable to THE NEW YORK TIMES
LONDON, April 6

'The death of the Earl of Carnarvon has revived interest in stories told concerning a mummy-case which once contained the mummy of a priestess of Amen-Ra, who died in Egypt 3,500 years ago and which is now in the British Museum. Is it really ill-omened? Can it bring misfortune to all who touch it? Sir Ernest Budge, keeper of Egyptian antiquities at the museum, laughs at those who suggest it, but the guides who show visitors round are not so sure.

In one of the principal rooms of the Egyptian section is a glass case containing a long row of mummy-cases. They are thousands of years old, but one stands out. Its bright coloring catches the eye of every passer-by. It looks almost as fresh as the day it left the painter's hand, and the figure which is its principal feature is extraordinarily life-like. There can be no doubt it is the portrait of the woman who once occupied the sarcophagus. She was a priestess of the great god Amen-Ra, and apart from that she must have been an extremely attractive and clever woman. Even today, after all these years, her portrait seems to retain that enigmatical smile which men associate with the Mona Lisa, and she appears to gaze mockingly at the idle sightseers as if he knew her secret power. And if legend be true, even to this day she has no objection to using it.

It was in 1864 that an Arab found the mummy-case and sold it to a wealthy traveler. Within a few weeks, so the story goes, he lost his money and died of a broken heart. Two of his servants who had handled the case died within a year. A third, who did not touch it, but made contemptuous remarks concerning it, lost his arm through a gunshot accident.

Malignancy in England
The mummy-case was brought to London and wherever it went carried misfortune with it, of which perhaps the most remarkable was the fate that befell a photographer. He took a picture of the case and when he came to develop the negative

received a horrifying shock. It was not a picture of a mere painting he had secured, but, so the story goes, a portrait of a living woman whose beautiful features had taken on a look of awful malignity.

The curse connected with the mummy-case became known, and as no buyer was forthcoming it was sent to the British Museum. The man who contracted to take it there died a week later and one of his helpers broke his leg the next day.

Again it was photographed by a well-known London firm and a strange chain of disasters befell the photographer. He first smashed his thumb, and when he got home found one of his children had fallen through a glass frame and had received dangerous injuries. The day he took the picture he cut his nose to the bone and dropped a valuable screen, rendering it quite useless.

Still the picture was taken and there was something uncanny about it. Its eyes seemed to glow with fire and those who saw it could not believe it could be anything but the portrait of a woman filled with a wild malignity.

So the old legend went and grew from year to year. W.T. Stead took great interest in it and publication of myths concerning it have invariably resulted in numberless letters to newspapers detailing how some bank holiday visitors to the museum had been attracted by the freshness of pigments on the mummy-case only to be victims sooner or later of such accidents as stumbling on entering a street car or breaking a mirror at home.

Most disasters, both public and private, seem to have been laid to the account of the beautiful priestess of Amen-Ra, and it was even said that the loss of the Titanic was due to her malign influence. An American, it was declared, had managed to purchase her coffin case from the Museum officials and was bringing her over to the United States on the Titanic. Naturally, the liner struck an iceberg with awful results. But even then its owner was unconvinced of his impiety in moving the mummy-case to the New World and with an enormous bribe induced some of the Titanic crew to save it. He lived to regret it, however, and at last aghast at the misfortunes it brought in its train to himself and his family he palmed it off on an innocent Canadian.

For some reason that gentleman wished to return it to Europe and shipped it on the Empress of Ireland. No one can deny that that ship sank in the St. Lawrence River somewhere, which is complete proof of what the priestess of Amen-Ra can do when she is thoroughly aroused.

Budge Explains it All

So goes the legendary lore, but now comes Sir Ernest Budge with a little common sense. Talking a few weeks ago to the Sunday Times he said the whole myth was founded on a series of misunderstandings. [sic] W.T. Stead and Douglas Murray told the story about another mummy which a lady put as an ornament in her drawing room. Next morning she found all her bric-a-brac smashed to pieces, and when her husband locked the mummy up in a cupboard in an upper room the servants declared they saw troops of beings ascending the stairs all night with lights in order to break all the crockery they could find, and resigned en masse the next day.

Just about the same time a man named Wheeler gave the priestess' coffin lid to the museum and Mr. Stead and Mr. Murray examined it and declared that to them it seemed the face of a portrait. It looked like a picture of a soul in torment, they said, and they wanted to hold a séance in the museum to see if they could do something to relieve the lady. But naturally the authorities did not agree.

The story got out and the public proceeded to identify the priestess of Amen-Ra with the crockery smashing mummy of the suburban drawing room. People have written from so far afield as New Zealand and Algiers enclosing money to place lilies at the foot of the coffin lid. The money has been acknowledged, but it has been put to the much more prosaic use of the general upkeep of the museum.

As for the Titanic story, Sir Ernest can only say that the museum has never parted with the lid, although during air raids it was removed for safety to the basement and it has, since it became a part of the national collection, never left the care of the museum.

Still its brilliant colors attract most careless visitors and anyone can hear all about its malignant power by approaching tactfully the nearest of the museum's attendants.

If I remember correctly one officer aboard the HMS Hampshire was said to carry a memento from the mummy when it sunk in the North Sea, killing all aboard (including Lord Kitchener).

The recent piece about Learmouth Garden brought back to me all those ideas about the occult powers of the ancient Egyptians and particularly how dangerous it is to disturb their dead. The so called 'Tutankhamen's Curse' is the most famous but there's another less known stories related by none other than Sir Ernest Wallis Budge, world-famous Egyptologist and British Museum Keeper which gave London perhaps the best collection of Middle Eastern antiquities in the world.

Not all Americans were so skeptical. The following was printed in the *American Photography* paper by the camera club of New York (Volume 4, 1910):

The curse of the malign mummy was not taken altogether seriously in some quarters: First there is the wonderful news, all freshly dished up, of that deadly mummy case in the British Museum. I have already written twice about it, and anyone who fancies chancing his luck by examining it will find it in the corner reached by turning sharp to the left on entering the last of the Egyptian rooms. By its side is the famous photograph of it. You will remember that the photographer, or his aunt or his cat, or somebody or something, died afterwards. This shows the rash folly of photographing anything. No one can dispute the statement that large numbers of people who have taken photographs have subsequently expired. We cannot be too careful. Anyone who exposes a plate on a mummy-case will certainly die after it.

Chapter 4

The Last Train Standing...

The history of the pharaoh's curse in the Western world takes an altogether more modern twist in the late 18th century with the building of British Museum station in Bury Place, which then sat between Tottenham Court Road and Chancery Lane underground stations on the then Central London Railway (CLR), now the Central line. The family of Benjamin Brown, one of a number of labourers working on the building of the station and the underground tunnel system, contacted me after a talk I presented in London in 2008. They told me an incredible tale that had remained within the family ever since the incidents took place. This is the first time the story has been printed.

It is hard to imagine the abysmal conditions for workers during construction of the underground railway network. The dust-filled air, lack of natural lighting and the foul smell from the unsanitary working environment was enough to make the hardiest of souls extremely ill. These were just a few of the issues facing this workforce on a daily basis. In late 1899, as the British Museum station was nearing completion, some of the labourers working there reported strange noises echoing through the tunnels, sounding like distressed humans, calling for help. Dismissing it as distorted natural sound from the surface, the men continued working. Within moments the sound grew louder, becoming clearer and turning into shrill, screeching screams. One of the men was so disturbed by the sound that he downed tools and walked into the darkness of a tunnel. The rest of his crew stopped work and stood waiting for their colleague to return. Once the man had entered the tunnel, the screaming stopped and all was quiet. Suddenly the platform and station area was filled with a cacophony of loud screams, which seemed to rush out of a tunnel as though pressure was being released. The five men clamped their hands over their ears in an attempt to silence the noise, which persisted for several minutes before suddenly stopping. Terrified, the men began shouting for their colleague, who was nowhere to be seen. Finally, after about fifteen minutes he emerged from the tunnel. His face was ashen and his eyes, wide open, stared directly in front of him. His hair had turned entirely white. The men sat him down, gave him water and tried to calm his frantic breathing. For a few moments the man could not speak, but he soon recovered sufficiently to describe what had happened in the tunnel.

The screaming had got louder the further into the tunnel he walked, until he saw a figure standing on the rail track in front of him. The image was blurred and appeared to be floating in mid-air! As he drew closer he saw it was a man wearing a golden headdress, which he described as being like a crown, but taller. The headdress seemed to be alive; it was coiled around the man's head and was moving very much like a snake. The man moved towards him: he had no eyes, just dark holes where his eyes once were, and his face was pale and white. The worker was transfixed as the figure moved closer to him: its hands outstretched and its long, bony fingers curled. Behind it he saw a procession of ghost-like apparitions in long flowing gowns, some wearing gold jewellery. The men looked as though they were slaves. The first apparition stopped a few feet before him and turned to face its followers. It addressed them in a foreign tongue and they stopped and looked at the lead figure. Suddenly the figure raised its left hand and held aloft the head of a large black dog, with blood dripping from it. The followers fell to their knees and began to chant some kind of mystical incantation, which the worker felt to be a prayer.

Unable to move or speak, the man watched as the lead figure removed its headdress, which had turned into a writhing snake, before pulling the bloodied dog's head over his own and snarling and roaring! Without warning a scream like that of a thousand cursed women began to fill the tunnel. The worker felt pain in his eardrums, which had started to bleed, but being unable to move he could do nothing to dampen the noise. The crowd of followers rose as one and disappeared before him, and the sound of the screaming moved past him and beyond towards the station platform area, leaving just him and the dog-headed being in the tunnel. The being moved slowly towards him until it was no more than a few inches from his face. He could smell the scent of death on its breath as it confronted him. Its eyes were black and like red-hot pokers searing into his own. Feeling he could move, he raised his hands to touch the head and try to remove it from the being, since part of him believed it was tomfoolery and he wanted to reveal the culprit. As he lifted his hands to the snout of the being, it snarled at him, its top lip revealing blood-stained teeth and fangs. The worker pulled at the head but it was fused to the human body it now sat upon. It moved forward, causing him to fall backwards, whereupon it sat on his chest. The hands, which had once been human, were now sharp claws. He knew he was about to die. As the figure looked down towards his heart he closed his eyes and began to pray for forgiveness for all of his sins. Moments later the figure was gone. It disappeared into thin air, allowing him to leave the tunnel and return to his colleagues. The man had no idea his hair had turned white, nor that he looked like a living corpse. He was taken to the surface and told to go home and rest.

Many of those who heard the story dismissed it as the product of exhaustion. Long hours in claustrophobic conditions could have caused the worker's mind to wander and his imagination to run riot. A few days later he was found dead in his East London home: he had hanged himself. He left a note explaining that he felt cursed by the souls of those murdered and left in the desert sands. No one understood the true meaning of the suicide note, and no one could explain why five other men had heard the screaming voices, nor why the man's hair had turned white, other than through fright! A ring found in the tunnel was thought to be the worker's and was taken to him before his suicide, by Benjamin Brown. However, he declared it wasn't his and appeared terrified by it. The ring was in the shape of a coiled serpent, a snake-like creature. The man told Brown that he had seen it on the hand of the mysterious figure before it morphed into a wild human dog-like creature. He told Brown to take the ring back to the tunnel and throw it as far inside as he could. Brown told no one about it, and did as he was asked. Over the weeks that followed, Brown left London and claimed to be possessed by an evil spirit that urged him to act in sinful manner. He would scream at invisible visions that he claimed stood before him and haunted his every living moment. He declared the worst of these to be a large black dog-headed man, menacingly holding a knife that dripped with blood.

Although this is an anecdote, the descriptions of the mysterious figure certainly resemble Anubis, the Egyptian god of the dead. When the British Museum station opened on 30 July 1900, only the handful of workers who had been employed there knew of the dark secret that existed within the tunnel. It remained that way until other sinister and unaccountable happenings began to occur there. Reports of black figures being seen in the station seemingly continued for several decades, right up until the station was officially closed on 24 September 1933. One CLR worker told me of countless incidents when, late at night, people would see movements in the shadows that followed them through the station, which only stopped when they exited completely or alighted a train departing from the station. One woman, who was standing on the station platform, described being approached by a foreign man who asked if she could help him find a ring he had dropped. He persuaded her to move to the platform edge. There she felt something pushing her from behind, forcing her onto the tracks. She screamed and the figure disappeared; all she could hear was a horrible wailing sound that filled the entire station platform. Realising she was alone, she felt in danger and ran back to the main concourse where she told the guard. Thinking her drunk or mad, he did nothing, until other travellers spoke of similar encounters.

On another occasion, a man who was alone on the platform was actually pushed onto the track. Looking up he saw a figure wearing an ornate headdress, sandals and a loincloth. He asked for help to climb out, but the figure stood with its arms folded, blocking his way. Running along the line he eventually managed to scramble back up onto the platform before any train arrived, and he left the station on the next train.

In 1912 three women came rushing into the main concourse hysterical; they had been terrified by what they saw. A man wearing a black dog's head had walked along the platform towards them. Thinking it was someone wearing fancy dress they laughed, but the creature snarled at them and tried to claw at one of women's coats,

50

tearing it. The women said the creature's breath smelt foul, like the smell of rotting flesh and death.

By 1913, for logistical reasons, CLR planned to close the British Museum station. Nearby Holborn station (opened in 1906) had made the British Museum station virtually redundant. The outbreak of the First World War delayed the closure and the station remained open. The vast majority of apparitions or incidents at the station relate to a dog-headed man, and almost all reports mention accompanying laughter or cackling sounds and female screams like that of a banshee. It wasn't long before supposition and imagination turned the incidents into something connected to the British Museum itself. It was suggested that the station was haunted by the wandering and restless spirit of Amen-Ra, whose mummy board was in the Egyptian Room. Talk of an underground tunnel that led from the station to the museum was popular. So numerous were the stories circulating about the cursed underground station, that *The Times* newspaper offered a reward to anyone who would spend the night alone in the station. There were no takers!

The London Underground has always denied any reports or suggestions that anything sinister ever happened at British Museum station. 'There are no ghosts, no dead Egyptian mummies, or weird dog-headed men roaming about the London underground, nothing other than our commuters.' Despite the denials, many people still claim to see and hear strange noises and sounds that are similar to the early reports, although now the sounds are being reported as being heard at Holborn station. I personally have obtained a number of reports of what can only be described as 'Anubis-like' creatures being seen in the tunnels at Holborn and banshee-like screaming being heard. Today's London is a multicultural society with all manner of clothing on display, so sightings of dog-headed men or Egyptian god figures are not as outlandish as they might once have been, although some do fit into the 'unexplained phenomenon' category. I asked the Metropolitan Police for any official reports into such incidents, historical or otherwise. They declined to comment, which does not help our research.

With trains no longer running into the station, in 1935 it became the setting for a comedy thriller feature film, *Bulldog Jack*, which used the basis of the legend and curse as its storyline, including the invention of a secret tunnel from the station directly to the Egyptian Room in the British Museum! The film opened in April 1935, and on the night of its première performance sinister goings-on were repeated. Two women disappeared at Holborn Station and were never found or seen again. The Metropolitan Police made no comment about such an incident, so there is no concrete evidence for the story. However, there does exist a story of a couple (Mr and Mrs Taylor) who witnessed the disappearance.

The Taylors had seen the women on the platform close to the tunnel entrance and had taken no real notice of them until they heard a scream from that direction. When they turned to see what had spooked the women, they were no longer there. Mr Taylor walked down to where the women had stood but saw nothing, so later told a guard what had happened. A search party was sent out into the tunnels and, at the now-closed British Museum station, strange scratch marks were found on the station walls. These appeared to be claw-like marks, but of a size that was as large as a human hand.

After the official closure of the British Museum station, the infrastructure remained in use until the 1960s as a military administrative office and emergency command post. During this period more strange goings-on occurred, with screams, shouting foreign voices and visions being witnessed by many of those working there. A civilian worker complained so frequently of the screaming women that he was forced to leave his employment. Another man who scoffed and dismissed talk of the station being cursed, and denied Egyptian curses, soon fell ill and died from the effects of tuberculosis.

The surface station was eventually demolished in 1989, completely preventing access to the station from street level. By this time, all the station platforms had been removed and the eastbound tunnel was used for storage by track engineers. The British Museum station is still mentioned or used as a backdrop in films, plays and novels, and was featured in the 1972 horror film *Death Line,* the Keith Lowe book *Tunnel Vision* and in the stage play *Pornography*. It is possibly London's most infamous underground station.

Chapter 5

The Curse of Cleopatra's Needle

The history of Cleopatra's Needle is indeed a magical one and deserves to be told and recounted in this volume. Some 700 miles beyond Cairo on the Nile, on the frontiers of Nubia, is the town of Syene or Assouan. In this area are the famed quarries of red granite called Syenite or Syenitic stone. About fifteen centuries before the Christian era, in the reign of Thutmose III, the obelisk now in London and a companion stone were quarried at Syene then placed on a huge raft and floated down the Nile to the sacred city of Heliopolis (referred to in the Bible as On). This was a city of temples dedicated to the worship of the sun. It is also regarded as a celebrated seat of learning and such exalted figures as Moses, Pythagoras and Plato and many Greek philosophers were students here.

On their arrival at Heliopolis the two obelisks were erected in front of the great temple of the sun, where they remained for fourteen centuries. These wonderful objects would have been gazed upon by Moses, Plato and many other historical figures. In later years the Roman emperor Augustus Caesar had the two obelisks taken down and moved from Heliopolis to Alexandria. During the journey, the road beneath the cart carrying the obelisk supposedly collapsed, revealing a hidden prehistoric tomb. Dozens of men are said to have died in the collapse. At Alexandria, the needles stood in front of the Caesarium (the Palace of the Caesars). They were put there seven years after the death of Cleopatra and, interestingly, their move to Alexandria had nothing to do with her. It seems most likely that the needles were named in memory of her.

The obelisks remained in Alexandria for a further fifteen centuries. Eventually, around 400 years ago, due to the ravages of time and natural elements, one of the obelisks fell to the ground and remained there, gradually becoming buried in the sands. During the 1798 'Battle of the Nile' Lord Nelson's fleet ambushed and defeated Napoleon's fleet while anchored off the coast of Alexandria. The fallen monument was viewed as a trophy to commemorate the victory and efforts were made to recover it to England, although the army lacked the resources to transport it. So it remained in Alexandria until the early part of the 19th century, when discussions were again held about recovering the monument from Egypt. By 1820, on the accession to the throne of King George IV, the monument was again offered to the British by the Egyptian ruler Mehemet Ali. Sadly, the gift was rejected. Later, in 1831, Mehemet Ali renewed his offer, this time to William IV. He promised to ship the monolith from Egypt to England without charge. Again the undoubted compliment and offer was declined! In 1849 politicians again discussed the opportunity to collect the obelisk and have it transported to London, although the opposition party warned 'That the obelisk was too much defaced to be worth renewal'. So it remained in Alexandria. In 1851 the topic was discussed once more; the outlay of £7,000 for transportation costs was deemed unacceptable to the public purse.

Eventually, the decision was made to collect the monolith, but government officials left the task to Sir William James Erasmus Wilson, who would subsidise the project. In 1877, Wilson paid a bond for the sum of £10,000 to Mr John Dixon, CE for the transportation and delivery of the monolith. A specially-designed craft was engineered to carry the obelisk at sea. The needle was encased in a watertight iron pontoon-type vessel, often referred to as 'cigar-shaped'. It was named *Cleopatra* and measured almost 100 feet in length. It had a vertical stem and stern, a rudder, two bilge keels, a mast for balancing sails, and a deck house. It was designed to be towed behind another vessel, the steam tug *Olga* (with Captain Booth at the helm), with Captain Carter and crew members aboard the *Cleopatra*. Both vessels set sail from Alexandria Harbour on 21 September 1877 bound for London.

For twenty days the voyage went as planned: the sailing was good and very few problems were encountered. The pontoon appeared relatively stable. Some of the crew were to later recall hearing strange moaning noises that were apparently 'human like'. At times there was the sound of rhythmic incantations in an unknown foreign language, but some crew members dismissed the sounds as the mind playing tricks on them. These men, however, were well used to the strange ways of the sea: they recognised the sounds of the wind and waters. It was also said that a curious suffocating atmosphere prevailed on both vessels, as though the men were in a dreamlike state.

Matters took a turn for the worse on 14 October 1877, when, as both vessels travelled through the Bay of Biscay, a violent storm erupted and the seas transformed from a manageable swell to huge waves that lashed over the vessels. The *Cleopatra* began to roll wildly, to such an extent that its safety and security became a real concern. The crews of both vessels fought desperately against the wind and waves in an attempt to maintain course and control, but the unrelenting storm was relentless in its battering. Eventually, after an epic battle that had lasted several hours, one end of the pontoon containing the obelisk disappeared below the surface, causing the opposite end to rise upright out of the water. The sinking and loss of the *Cleopatra* seemed certain.

The crew continued to frantically battle against the elements. Six volunteer crewmen – William Askin, Michael Burns, James Gardiner, William Donald, Joseph Benbow and William Patan – all died during the struggle with the raging seas. Captain Carter and five other crew members were fortunate to be rescued and were taken on board the *Olga*.

Shortly after midnight the situation became so desperate that the decision was made to cut the *Cleopatra* free of the *Olga*, and allow it to sink of its own accord. It was with great reluctance that Captain Booth, believing the battle was lost, abandoned the *Cleopatra* to her fate and prepared to make sail for England minus the obelisk.

Unknown to anyone onboard the *Olga*, however, instead of sinking the pontoon somehow righted itself. Against all odds, it remained afloat for a further sixty hours, when it was eventually located and picked up by the steamer *Fitzmaurice* and safely towed to the port of Vigo, Spain, where it was kept awaiting collection.

In England, a tugboat was especially adapted to sail to Spain to collect the *Cleopatra* and bring it to London. There were further stories of mysterious voices, wailing and incantations being heard by crew members during this journey, but no further calamities occurred. So the Cleopatra eventually arrived in the River Thames, where it was towed to its final resting position by the paddle tug *Anglia*, under the command of Captain David Glue. Crowds of people stood on the banks of the river to witness the spectacle; in Kent, schoolchildren were given a 'day off' to watch the *Cleopatra* pass by.

Eventually, on 12 September 1878, the needle was erected in its current location on the Thames Embankment. Two bronze Sphinxes sit at its base, facing the wrong way (it is claimed that Queen Victoria thought this pose was more aesthetically pleasing). They should be facing away from the obelisk (not towards it), to protect and defend it. These statues were added later, having been designed by George John Vulliamy and created at the Ecclestone Iron Works in Pimlico in 1881. They bear the inscription 'The good god, Thuthmosis III, given life.'

Two earthenware jars were buried in the front part of the pedestal beneath the Needle. Alongside them, it is said, were buried:

Photographs of twelve English beauties of the day
A box of hairpins
A box of cigars
Several tobacco pipes
A baby's bottle
Some children's toys
A shilling razor
A hydraulic jack and some samples of the cable used in the erection
A 3 inch bronze model of the monument
A complete set of British coins
A rupee
A portrait of Queen Victoria
A written history of the strange tale of the transport of the monument
Plans on vellum
A translation of the inscriptions
Copies of the Bible in several languages

A copy of Whitaker's *Almanac*
A *Bradshaw Railway Guide*, a map of London
Copies of ten daily newspapers

As for the vessel *Cleopatra*, her task was complete, and she was sent for scrap!

There is a definite belief that Cleopatra's Needle is cursed, which is reinforced by the unfortunate circumstances that surround its trip to London. A high number of deaths by suicide have occurred in its vicinity; it seems to be a magnet for sinister activity. It is claimed by some that the curse was placed on the monolith by the pharaoh Rameses II. He modified the original hieroglyphics on the needle in around 1300 BC, changing the meaning from prayers to Ra the sun god, to prayers about himself! The self-proclaimed world's most evil man, Aleister Crowley, was totally convinced that the Rameses II carvings contained a magical spell that preserved the soul of the dead pharaoh within the stone of the needle.

Crowley was obsessed with the monument and was known to have acquired a human skeleton that he regularly took to the needle in the dark of night. There he would feed animal blood to the skeleton, in the belief that it would return to life with Rameses II's reincarnated spirit. There have also been reports of deep, mocking laughter coming from within the Needle, and sightings of a dark shadowy figure majestically moving around the Needle's base that disappears when approached by a living human entity. Others have heard and seen six shadow figures wailing at the foot of the monument, their sobbing sounds turning into desperate screams of anguish. These figures, many claim, are those of the six crewmen who lost their lives attempting to bring the Needle to London.

Believers in the curse claim that Cleopatra's Needle was the first monument in London to be hit during a First World War air raid. A mounted plaque on the Sphinx to the right of the obelisk (as one faces the Thames), incorrectly states:

THE SCARS THAT DISFIGURE THE PEDESTAL OF THE OBELISK, THE BASES OF THE SPHINXES, AND THE RIGHT HAND SPHINX, WERE CAUSED BY FRAGMENTS

OF A BOMB DROPPED IN THE ROADWAY CLOSE TO THIS
SPOT, IN THE FIRST RAID ON LONDON BY GERMAN
AEROPLANES A FEW MINUTES BEFORE MIDNIGHT ON
TUESDAY 4TH SEPTEMBER 1917.

The detail on the plaque is wrong: the air raid of 4 September 1917 was not the first raid on London by German aeroplanes. Gotha bombers had carried out daylight raids on the city during June and July 1917, and there had been a further daylight bombing of the capital on 28 November 1916. The first night raid carried out by German aeroplanes took place on 6 May 1917.

A further apparition is often seen by the obelisk at night or early in the morning: a naked man who runs from behind the monument and jumps into the dirty cold water of the Thames. A loud splash is heard as the waters engulf him without any sign of surface disturbance. No one knows who the spirit represents. It is said he was a late Victorian disciple of Rameses II who was driven insane by the spell of the Needle; he turned into a killer and ended his own life within the shadow of the Needle. The shadowy figure was believed to be the serial killer known as the Thames Torso Killer: the crimes associated with that individual are said to have stopped in 1889.

In 1993 a more amazing, yet equally sinister claim was made about the Needle, this time relating to what might be buried beneath it: sacred and magical tools that originated from within the Great Pyramid of King Cheops in Egypt. It was claimed by scholar and researcher Robert Bauval that in 1872, civil engineer Waynman Dixon was asked to go to Egypt to carry out survey work at the pyramids. There he visited the Great Pyramid and began to investigate one of its large internal rooms, the Queen's Chamber. During his investigation he discovered a tunnel and began to explore it. Some six feet along its length he came across three mysterious ritual objects which he removed. They were:

A hook-like bronze implement known as a pesash-kaf; this instrument was used by ancient Egyptian surveyors, possibly during the construction of major buildings including the Pyramids. It was also used by ancient priests to open the mouths of the dead, thus allowing the corpse to 'breathe' and be reborn into the next life.

A granite or dolomite sphere about the size of a cricket ball, believed to have been used during pyramid construction as an implement to smooth rough stone.

A five-inch length of cedar wood which was a small part of a larger item. It had been broken off and was believed to be a builder's measuring rod.

Waynman Dixon's brother John, who was a prominent British Freemason, arrived in Cairo a short time after the find had been made and was given the relics by his brother. Both men then travelled to Alexandria to examine the great obelisk that later became known as Cleopatra's Needle, which they wanted to bring to England. It is worth noting that Egyptian pyramids and obelisks were of great importance to Freemasons a century ago. Many believe that the Great Pyramid was an ancient Masonic temple! Sir Erasmus Wilson, who put up the money to bring the Needle to London, was himself a leading British Freemason and engaged John Dixon to arrange its passage. Dixon also designed the pedestal upon which the Needle stands, and the suggestion is that he placed the ancient sacred relics taken from the Great Pyramid within the pedestal.

A group of tourists visiting London in 2012 contacted the author to explain a strange occurrence that had taken place at night next to the Needle. The group, consisting of four women and five men, had been walking along the Embankment and had collectively heard the sound of singing voices. As they neared the obelisk, the sounds grew louder and were described as being not dissimilar to a group of men chanting. The sounds stopped and one of the men saw a movement right next to the Needle. It was, he believed, the form of a dog-headed man crouched over a laid-out corpse. The figure looked as if it was carrying out some operation on the head of the body. In one hand it appeared to hold a stick-like object. As he called to others in the group to look, they all saw the crouched figure move to a standing position, then disappear inside the stone needle. Rushing to the scene they could find no evidence to support what they had all witnessed, so they set about trying to disprove it as a trick of the light. No matter how hard they tried, no rational explanation was obvious. Shadows from the road did not cast shapes or forms in the area where the sighting took place, and there was no chanting noise.

Somewhat disturbed by the incident, they opted to believe that it must have been some form of trickery and they continued on their way. They were hardly twenty-five yards from the Needle when one of the group looked back and again saw the shadow of a tall dog-headed man appear, and bend down over what looked like a prostrate human form. Within moments, the chanting sound had resumed.

I have visited Cleopatra's Needle on the Thames Embankment countless times and carried out various lighting tests to check what shadows are cast and how. I have been unable to recreate anything like the shadows witnessed by the group of tourists, even deliberately it is virtually impossible to mimic what they saw. I questioned each member of the group and asked them to describe the image, particularly the dog-headed man. The sketches produced were almost identical and are shockingly similar to Anubis, although no one in the group claimed or professed to know anything about Cleopatra's Needle or ancient Egypt. They were in London for a week's holiday.

As for the chanting noise the group heard? Well, the River Thames and passing boat traffic are just a few feet from the Embankment walk, so it could be that noise was emanating from a vessel. Or the sound could have come from road and vehicular noise; in-car entertainment systems are played loudly by some drivers. On its own noise or sounds aren't strong evidence of mysterious goings-on. But in conjunction with the sightings it certainly seems sinister.

I do not believe in coincidence and for me there are too many different anecdotes and details about Cleopatra's Needle for them all to be totally unfounded. If you include recorded deaths, suicides and historical anecdotes, somewhere in the region of seventy deaths are connected to Cleopatra's Needle. That's far too many for me to readily dismiss as coincidence or accidental. So is Cleopatra's Needle in London cursed? I leave it to you to decide!

Chapter 6

The Dog-Headed Men

The archetypal Western image of an Egyptian god is that of a human form with an animal head, usually that of jackal or dog, like Anubis, although it can be a human with a bird head, such as Thoth. This isn't an image that has been deliberately inflicted upon us by our modern-day culture but rather, through the ancient drawings found inside tombs and at temples that were produced by the Egyptians themselves. There exists a veritable pantheon of such strange and curious looking entities, all of which were worshipped by the people and the great pharaohs themselves. Yet such creatures not only feature in Egyptian culture, but in other civilisations too. The creature we are concerned with here is the dog-headed man, which often appears in tales of curses. A dog-headed creature is sometimes referred to as a cynocephalus, meaning a two-legged human being with the head of a dog. In many cultures such creatures are viewed as savage and a threat. The most infamous of all dog-headed men is the Egyptian god Anubis, yet it was a Greek physician, Ctesias, who first documented such beings in the fifth century BC. He claimed that many such people lived in caves in the mountains of India, communicating by barking at one another and eating nothing but raw meat. He went on to state that these beings kept sheep and fought with swords, bows and spears that were exchanged for amber from fruit trees. He wrote:

The Kynokephaloi living on the mountains do not practise any trade but live by hunting. When they have killed an animal they roast it in the sun. They also rear numbers of sheep, goats, and asses, drinking the milk of the sheep and whey made from it. They eat the fruit of the Siptakhora, whence amber is procured, since it is sweet. They also dry it and keep it in baskets, as the Greeks keep their dried grapes. They make rafts which they load with this fruit together with well-cleaned purple flowers and 260 talents of amber, with the same quantity of the purple dye, and 1000 additional talents of amber, which they send annually to the king of India. They exchange the rest for bread, flour, and cotton stuffs with the Indians, from whom they also buy swords for hunting wild beasts, bows, and arrows, being very skilful in drawing the bow and hurling the spear. They cannot be defeated in war, since they inhabit lofty and inaccessible mountains. Every five years the king sends them a present of 300,000 bows, as many spears, 120,000 shields, and 50,000 swords.

They do not live in houses, but in caves. They set out for the chase with bows and spears, and as they are very swift of foot, they pursue and soon overtake their quarry. The women have a bath once a month, the men do not have a bath at all, but only wash their hands. They anoint themselves three times a month with oil made from milk and wipe themselves with skins. The clothes of men and women alike are not skins with the hair on, but skins tanned and very fine. The richest wear linen clothes, but they are few in number. They have no beds, but sleep on leaves or grass. He who possesses the greatest number of sheep is considered the richest, and so in regard to their other possessions. All, both men and women, have tails above their hips, like dogs, but longer and more hairy. They are just, and live longer than any other men, 170, sometime 200 years.

Elsewhere, such creatures were frequently recorded. Herodotus, a Greek historian of the 5th century BC, reported:

For the eastern region of Libya, which the Nomads inhabit, is low-lying and sandy as far as the Triton river; but the land west of this, where the farmers live, is exceedingly mountainous and wooded and full of wild beasts. In that country are the huge snakes and the lions, and the elephants and bears and asps, the

horned asses, the Kunokephaloi (Cynocephali) (Dog-Headed)
and the Headless Men that have their eyes in their chests, as
the Libyans say, and the wild men and women, besides many
other creatures not fabulous.

The Greek Aelian (*On Animals*), when writing about natural history
in the 2nd century AD, wrote:

In the same part of India as the [crimson-dye] beetles, are
born the Kynokephaloi (Cynocephali) (Dog-Heads), as they
are called – a name which they owe to their physical
appearance and nature. For the rest they are of human shape
and go about clothed in the skins of beasts; and they are upright
and injure no man; and though they have no speech they howl;
yet they understand the Indian language. Wild animals are their
food, and they catch them with the utmost ease, for they are
exceedingly swift of foot; and when they have caught them
they kill and cook them, not over a fire but by exposing them
to the sun's heat after they have shredded them into pieces.
They also keep goats and sheep, and while their food is the
flesh of wild beasts, their drink is the milk of the animals they
keep. I have mentioned them along with brute beasts, as is
logical, for their speech is inarticulate, unintelligible, and not
that of man.

After traversing the Egyptian oasis one is confronted for
seven whole days with utter desert. Beyond this live the human
Kynoprosopoi (Cynoprosopi) (Dog-Faces) along the road that
leads to Aithiopia (Ethiopia). It seems that these creatures live
by hunting gazelles and antelopes; further, they are black in
appearance, and they have the head and teeth of a dog. And
since they resemble this animal, it is very natural that I should
mention them here [in a book on Animals]. They are however
not endowed with speech, but utter a shrill squeal. Beneath
their chin hangs down a beard; we may compare it with the
beards of Drakones, and strong and very sharp nails cover
their hands. Their whole body is covered with hair – another
respect in which they resemble dogs. They are very swift of foot

and know the regions that are inaccessible: that is why they appear so hard to capture.

It occurs to me now to mention the following additional facts relating to Kynokephaloi (Cynocephali) [thought to derive from travellers' accounts of baboons]. If a Kynokephalos finds some edible object with a shell on it (I mean almonds, acorns, nuts) its strips the shell off and cleans it out, after first breaking it most intelligently, and it knows that the contents are good to eat but that the outside is to be thrown away. And it will drink wine, and if boiled or cooked meat is served to it, it will eat its fill; and it likes well-seasoned food, but food boiled without any care it dislikes. If it wears clothes, it is careful of them; and it does everything else that I have described. If you put it while still tiny to a woman's breast, it will suck the milk like a baby.

In Europe, dog-headed men are known as Cynocephalus, the Greek word for a sacred Egyptian baboon that has the face of a dog. The name Kynokephalos means dog-headed, from 'kuôn', a dog, and 'kephalos', head. The Church has endorsed the existence of such beings: Saint Augustine made mention of the moral laws of the dog-headed men, and Saint Christopher is often depicted as having a dog's head. When in this form he led a sinful life, but once baptised he transformed into an entirely human being, complete with human head. In the legend of King Arthur, he and his army fight and defeat a band of dog-headed soldiers in the mountains surrounding Edinburgh, Scotland.

Over the years, sightings of dog-headed creatures have occurred in the most bizarre of climates and places. In the 1980s in Wisconsin, USA, several witnesses described creatures ranging from approximately five to seven feet tall, powerful and muscular, covered in fur, with large fangs and the head of a wolf or German Shepherd dog. This creature is often referred to as the 'Beast of Bray Road', and it has been described as a living, breathing being. In Michigan there have been over 500 recorded sightings of dog-headed men since the phenomenon was first mentioned on a local radio station in 1989. Often said to be a shape-shifter, it was also known to growl in a deep

An Egyptian relief, depicting Anubis preparing the dead body for its journey into the afterlife.

Egyptian relief,
icting Anubis
municating with a
raoh.

A statue of Anubis, which stood guard in the tomb of King Tutankhamun.

Rare film poster depicting how
the Western World viewed
Egyptian mummies.

Howard Carter opening the final entrance within
King Tutankhamun's tomb.

A rare copy of Lord
Caernarvon's death
certificate.

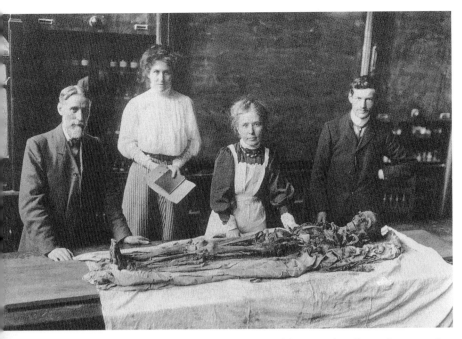

...inent Egyptologist, Dr Margaret Murray who believed in Egyptian Curses'unwrapping ...ummy.

Egyptian relief showing the body of a dead pharaoh being prepared for its journey into afterlife.

The inner entrance to King Tutankhmun's tomb - this had unofficially been entered Carter and Caernavon prior to its official opening. The access hole being covered by re and other items found within the tomb. The Egyptian authorities were unaware that Ca et all had entered the tomb.

The mummified head of an Egyptian ruler.

An early image of an unknown Egyptian selling mummies taken from their tombs.

Egyptian relied showing the God Osiris sat on his throne.

fferent image of a mummy
g prepared for the afterlife.

The Pyramids of Giza.

The form of a Scarab
beetle on a crafted
necklace.

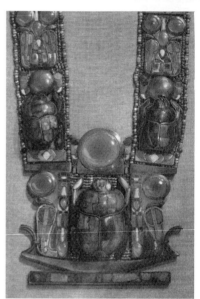

The Sphynx.

An early depiction of the Curse of the Pharaoh, showing a Mummy coming to life to kill the living.

Unwrapping a Royal Mummy was viewed as entertainment in the Victorian era.

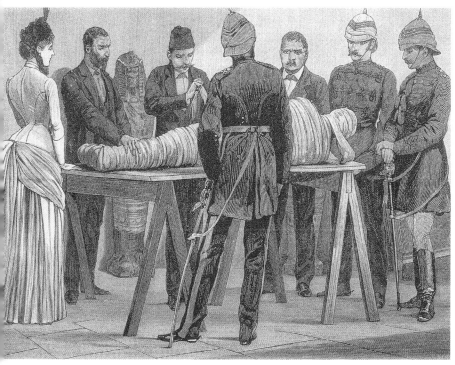

King Tutankhamun'
Royal Death Mask.

The 'Weighing of the Heart Ceremony' the final challenge facing the dead Pharaoh or
journey to the afterlife.

guttural tone. In 1992 a gravedigger found a stone with an intricate stone carving of a Pictish dog-headed man.

Could these beings ever have really existed? Or are they myths or stories promulgated since ancient times that have changed over time? No skeletal remains of dog-headed humans have ever been found. Yet the widespread myths do make one wonder where all these stories came from.

To return to the Egyptian dog-headed men, in Egyptian art the gods are often depicted in therianthropic form – human-like but with animal heads, such as Anubis, the cat-headed Bastet, or the ibis-headed Thoth. Accordingly, Anubis was shown with a jackal/dog-like head because the jackal/dog was associated with the necropolis. Such creatures were often seen roaming these districts in their natural form, thus the association with death and the underworld and so Anubis became a god of the dead. There are many other well-known gods with animal heads or bodies. The sphinxes all have human heads and lion bodies; Hathor is human in form but is depicted with cow's ears and horns. Taweret was a hybrid of a hippopotamus, crocodile and lioness. A twelfth-century hymn from the time of Ramesses III describes a god as 'divine power with hidden faces and mighty majesty, who has hidden his name and keeps his image secret, whose being was not known at the beginning of time.' An Egyptian text, known as Papyrus Leiden, dating from the thirteenth century, contains a somewhat curious verse: 'All gods are three: Amun, Re and Ptah, who have no equal. He hides his name as Amun, he appears as Re, his body is Ptah.'

It is clear that the Egyptians did not believe they had a whole race of dog or animal-headed creatures living among them. Such beings in ancient Egypt were regarded as gods, and were often feared. When these gods went anywhere and had cause to leave their temples they were usually borne on shoulder-supported carry-chairs that took many forms but were essentially boats. The idea that the gods were looking down on people and had the ability to move through large crowds without interference made them all the more superior. Small effigies of the gods were often purchased and kept in people's homes, where they were worshipped as much as the actual god itself. A number of texts advise us that the gods were often believed to descend from on high to dwell in images of themselves, which allowed their worshippers to interact with them.

Carved on the walls of the temple of Horus at Edfu is this inscription:

> *He comes down from heaven day by day*
> *in order to see his image upon his great throne.*
> *He descends upon his image*
> *and unites himself with his cult image.*

The gods also inhabited animal forms. The Apis bull at Memphis was treated as a living image of a god. It was pampered and groomed daily and consulted for oracles, and his mother was revered as an embodiment of Isis. When both creatures passed away they were treated with the same reverence as they were in life. They were mummified and were often spoken of as having become 'an Osiris'. Throughout Egyptian history there is evidence of animal worship and the mummification of a diverse range of creatures, such as baboons, cats, dogs, crocodiles, fish and beetles.

Herodotus records that in many Egyptian villages animals, birds or fish considered sacred to their local god were never sacrificed or eaten. Many Egyptian texts refer to the love their gods had for different animals. A hymn to Amun says:

> *Thou art the only one, the creator of all that is. From whose eye men came forth. From whose mouth the gods originated. Who creates the herbs which the cattle live on... Who creates that which the fish in the river live on. And the birds in the air. Who gives breath to the chicken in the egg. Who maintains the young of the snake. Who creates the nourishment of the gnat. And also of the worms and the fleas. Who cares for the mice in their hole and keeps alive the insects in every tree.*

While there remained a healthy respect for the animals of the gods, it is most unlikely that ancient Egyptians were pure vegetarians, and even if this was the case, it was for ethical reasons. In most instances, particularly among the poor and impoverished, the only reason meat wasn't eaten was because they couldn't afford it. From this, we can conclude that when the Egyptians saw their gods in dreams or in visions, they expected them to be like that in reality, human, animal or combination of both. In another display of reverence to the gods and animals, priests would don masks of the gods during certain ceremonies and celebrations; in essence the dressing up and portrayal was like them becoming the god itself. The masks were almost always the animal version of the god. The example of Anubis again springs to mind: it was during the mummification process that Anubis appeared to help mummify the body. The transformation itself is meant to represent a hybrid being, and not a human wearing a mask. In tombs, the statues of animals would be present to ward off evil intent and to deter anyone, such as tomb robbers, from entering that sacred place. Some animal effigies were strategically placed as guardians of the tomb, and the belief that in the underworld these creatures would spring into life and attack intruders was common. Death played a very important part in the lives of ancient Egyptians, and that animals were involved in the all-important preparations to the body, making it ready for the afterlife, speaks volumes about how they trusted and believed in animals' magic and wisdom. The Egyptians were no race of dog-headed men, but they did believe in the magical power of animals and how potent a force that could be in death.

Chapter 7

A Fate Worse Than Death

We start this chapter with an authentic 12th Dynasty Egyptian ghost story, taken from a writing known as *The Instruction of King Amenemhat I,* which was recorded by the early Egyptian writer Khety. The writing survives in fragmented and damaged papyrus form, but it also appears on wooden tablets and painted onto shards of pottery, thereby providing a more detailed retelling. As a result of his brutal assassination by his own staff and bodyguards, the ghost of the first 12th Dynasty pharaoh King Amenemhat I is claimed to have returned from the dead to visit his son and successor (Senusret I, also referred to as Sesostris I) to warn him to be aware of traitors in his midst. 'Listen to what I tell you so you may rule and govern well, and increase well-being!' He warns his son and heir against 'nobodies, whose plot remains hidden', and instructs him to 'trust no-one, neither a brother nor a friend; do not raise up for yourself intimate companions, for nothing is to be gained from them.' The ghost then describes his own murder:

It happened after supper, when night had come, as I rested peacefully for an hour, weary on my bed. As my heart turned to sleep the weapons of my protection were turned against me. I awoke fighting to find the bodyguards attacking. If only I had been quick enough and seized my weapons I would have made the cowards retreat at once! But none are might in the night and none can stand alone without a helper close beside. And all this happened while I was without you, before the courtiers knew I would hand everything over to you, before I had been able to sit with you and tell you of my plans. For I had not

prepared for this, had not foreseen the treachery of servants!
Senusret my son! I must leave you now and turn away. But you
are always in my heart and my eyes will always see you! My
child of a happy hour! I have established a beginning and wish
to plan the future, giving you the contents of my heart. You are
my likeness, and wear the white crown of your divine father.
Everything is as it should be. Fight for all the wisdom the heart
knows – for you will need it with you always.

The human race existed in Egypt for thousands of years before any form of mummification was introduced into funereal rites during the 4th Dynasty. As a culture, the Egyptians have always held a deep fascination with death, indeed, it is known from relics found in their graveyards, that the early Nagada civilisation developed a cult of the dead. The tombs were made of trenches dug out in the desert sands and were generally oval or rectangular in shape. The corpse lay on its left side, knees drawn up under the chin, with the head facing the south and the face turned to the west. The remains were generally covered in goat skin or some form of reed or rush matting. The early Egyptians believed that everything possessed a *ka* (spirit), the *khu* (the soul) and the *khat* (the body itself). Like many early races, the Egyptians believed the shadow to be a genuine representation of the soul, and others believed in the association of the *khaybet* (the shadow) with the *ka* (the spirit) and *sahu* (the mummy). The physical heart was known as *hati* and was seen as central to intelligence, and its spirit was called *ab*. They believed that the human personality combined both body and spirit. Tomb scenes often show the birth of kings with the royal baby represented by two figures: the visible body and the invisible double. The *ka* began at birth and continued to live on after death. The *ka*, it was believed, could leave the human body during sleep or while the subject lay in a trance. It then wandered about and visited people and places, and its experiences remained in the memory.

Early races such as the Negada buried their dead crouched in shallow graves in the belief that the ka remained beside the body until the flesh decayed, when it either ceased to be or haunted the cemetery. There was also a period of secondary internment, where the remains were reinterred and the skeletal bones placed in some order.

Dismemberment was commonly practised and some graves indicate that decapitation had occurred after death. A sacred book refers to mutilation of dead bodies: 'I shall not be destroyed – my head will not be cut off, nor my tongue taken out, nor will the hair of my head or my eyebrows be shaved off. My body will endure for all time.' As time passed, great importance was placed on the survival of the body and keeping it as intact as possible, and so the creation of more secure and stronger tombs became necessary. The walls of the grave began to change from having mud-coated linings, to being formed with branches and clay, and an early type of wooden lid covered the grave opening. All of this was to ensure the corpse suffered no crush damage through the collapsing of supporting walls originally made of earth and sand.

These early graves developed into unbaked brick-lined tombs, in which various chambers were gradually introduced, forming rooms with clearly defined space that separated the corpse from different areas that housed offerings to the gods, and necessities for the afterlife such as furniture. The design became so complex that the use of clay bricks and branches as a lining was no longer seen as safe or secure, so flat stone slabs, offering greater strength and resistance to unwanted intruders, were introduced into the infrastructure. Tombs often contained secret chambers which were deliberately difficult to access and hidden from the sight line of any intruder. To make access more difficult, entrance passages or shafts leading to the tombs were blocked with stone slabs and mounds of rubble as the funerary priests retreated from the tomb. Blind passages and trap doors were created and hidden holes and deep wells built into the tomb to trap any. In some instances, carefully placed wires were rigged to decapitate intruders. If that wasn't sufficient, the threat of poison being used in the coating of tomb, or in powders that were released into the air when stones were disturbed, might be sufficient to deter all but the most desperate tomb robber. Eventually, the tombs retreated into deeper underground rooms, the dead being carefully lowered into the tomb down a mined shaft that was later sealed with stones and sand. Above ground, the entire tomb was covered with a mastaba, a large rectangular embankment that was faced with limestone, inside which were two rooms. One of these is often referred to as the chapel, and was decorated with scenes of daily Egyptian life that was common to the deceased. Here, it was believed, the *ka* could enter and enjoy time as though it was still in the land of the living. The second room was known as the Serdab, and here a statue which resembled the dead person stood. This statue was important, because not only was it believed to communicate with the outside world, but it was also there to assist in the reincarnation of the *ka*. Over time, the burial custom evolved and the dead were laid on their backs, with the body fully extended, but no effort was made to preserve the body from decay, though offerings were placed in the tombs.

Eventually, by about 2700BC, large stone tombs were introduced and the bodies of the dead were mummified. The belief was that the *ka* would return and cause the dead to rise again, or that the existence of the soul in the underworld depended upon there being an intact body on earth. Embalming became common practice throughout Egypt. The embalmers were licensed to practise and possessed some surgical skills, but the quality of their work depended upon the money being spent. In an attempt to extract as much money as possible from grieving relatives, mock mummies were shown to clients in order to determine an agreeable mummification process and a price. The cheapest means of embalming was to inject a chemical preparation before the body was covered with nitre. At the end of seventy days, the intestines were drawn out. Nothing else remained other than skin and bones, the flesh having been eaten away by the nitre. This was all the poor could afford.

The most expensive embalming offered more care and attention to detail. The brain was extracted through the nostril after chemical infusion using an instrument made of palm and bamboo. This tool, measuring about ten inches in length, would be twisted inside the brain, wrapping brain matter around it, which was then pulled through the nasal cavity. A stone knife made an incision on one side of the body. The heart, liver, lungs and intestines were drawn out, and, after being cleansed, they were steeped in palm wine and sprinkled with rich perfume. Tiny sacks of natron were packed inside the body cavity to help dry it out. Once the body had dried, it was stuffed with powdered myrrh, cassia and resins, and sewn up. It was then covered with nitre for seventy days. Then it was washed all over and carefully wrapped in bandages that had been dipped in a strong gum. The intestines were placed in four canopic jars, the lids of which had the forms of four protecting gods, the four sons of Horus who represented north, south, east and west. Amset, with a human face, who guarded the stomach and large intestines; Duamutef, with a jackal's head, who guarded lungs and heart; and Kebeh-senuf, the hawk-headed, who guarded the liver and gall bladder. These jars were placed in a chest and deposited in the tomb. The organs they contained were those that were believed to have caused various sins to be committed. It is interesting to note how a nineteenth-century examination of a mummy, by the French archaeologist Gaston Camille Charles Maspero, was recorded in comparison to more modern procedures. Then the examination concentrated on appearance. Maspero was a Director of Antiquities at the Egyptian museum in Cairo, and was one of the first individuals to recognise the issue of the illegal export of Egyptian antiquities by visitors, collectors, and paid agents of the major museums across the globe. Sensationally, Maspero had two Egyptian brothers (Abd al-Russul) arrested for stealing mummies and artifacts from tombs. The men were held and suffered physical torture before finally confessing, in July 1881, to stealing many royal mummies at Deir el-Bahari. As a result, the bodies of the pharaohs Seti I, Amenhotep I, Thutmose III and Ramesses II, in sarcophagi, were recovered from a place close to the village and moved to Cairo. So it was that Maspero was able to investigate further the mummy of Ramesses II. On 1 June 1886 he recorded:

The first layer of cloth was removed successively a strip of material, about eight inches wide, wound round the body, then a second shroud sewn together and kept in place by narrow strips attached at intervals, then two thicknesses of bandaging and a piece of fine linen stretched from the head to toe. A picture of the goddess Naut, about three foot high, was drawn on the latter in red and black as prescribed in the ritual. A fresh bandage was placed under this amulet, then a layer of pieces of linen folded in squares, and stained with the bituminous matter the embalmers had used. When this last wrapping was removed, Ramesses II was revealed. He was tall (nearly six foot after embalming), well made, and perfectly symmetrical. His head was elongated and small in proportion to his body, and the top of his skull was completely bald. His hair, which was thin over his temples, became thicker towards his neck and fell in smooth straight locks about two inches long; it had been white when he died but was stained light yellow by the perfumes. His eyebrows jutted out from a low narrow forehead. He had thick white lashes, small close-set eyes, a long thin nose, hooked like a Roman and slightly flattened at the end by the weight of the wrappings, hollow temples, prominent cheekbones, rounded protruding ears with a delicate fold to the edge and holes pierced in the lobes for earrings, a strong and powerful jaw, and a very high chin. His mouth was wide open and had thick fleshy lips; it was filled with blackish paste, and when some of this was removed with a chisel we could see a few well-worn teeth which were quite fragile in spite of their white well-kept appearance. His moustache and beard, which were sparse and carefully shaved during his life, had grown either during his last illness or after his death. The hairs were white like those on his head and eyebrows, but coarse and spiky and barely a tenth of an inch long. His skin was a sickly yellow, caked with black stuff. His mask gave us a good idea of his facial expression when he was alive: he had unintelligent features which bordered on the animal, but they were coupled with a proud and determined air of sovereign majesty. The rest of the body was equally well preserved, but had kept its original appearance so well because the flesh had shrunk, and his neck for instance was no thicker than his spine. His chest was ample, his shoulders held high his arms crossed on his chest, and he had long delicate hands reddened with henna, with very beautiful nails cut level with the flesh and cared for like a kept woman's. There was a gaping wound on his left flank where the embalmers had taken out the viscera. His genital organs had been removed with the aid of a sharp instrument, and according to custom must have been buried separately in the hollow interior of a wooden figure of Osiris. His thighs and legs were emaciated, with long thin feet, rather flat, rubbed with henna, like his hands. His bones were weak and fragile and the muscles had atrophied through senile decay; indeed we know that Ramesses II reigned for a number of years with his father Seti I and then for seventy-two years alone, so he was nearly a hundred when he died.

Moving back to the funerary rituals, once the body was carried back to the dead person's home, it was placed in a large coffin which was shaped in human form, inscribed with magic charms and decorated with sacred symbols and figures of gods and goddesses. The face of the dead individual would be carved on the lid; in Roman times it would be painted on. Once ready, the internment could take place. The funeral procession, as it is today, was a solemn affair with all family members being present, as women mourners wailed aloud on the funerary route to the cemetery. The mummy, in its sealed coffin, was drawn along on a kind of sledge. On arrival at the tomb, the coffin was set up on its end, always facing the south. The ceremony was carried out by the chief mourner, whose role it was to recite the ritual from a prepared papyrus roll. Two females representing both Isis and Nepthys were present, and the ceremony was a replication of the scene when the god Osiris had his dismembered body restored by his wife after death and prepared for burial. At this stage the body had to be instructed on how to reach Egyptian heaven; it was to travel a long and arduous journey that could only be completed by use of magic formulae. These formulae were secret and were spoken into the corpse's ear. To make doubly sure the corpse would remember the instructions, the formulae were etched into the coffin, and also the walls of the tomb. It later became the custom to write this on papyrus rolls, which could be laid in the coffin or placed within the mummy bandages.

The coffin was then lowered down the grave shaft into a secret chamber, where an image of the dead had been placed, along with clothing, food, wine, a weapon, ornaments, perfumes and household possessions and even furniture. The entrance was then closed up and sealed. The cult of Osiris believed that heaven was the double of the Delta region. Before this could be reached the soul must travel a weary journey that was fraught with countless dangers. The paradise of Aalu, as it was known, was situated on the west bank of the Nile, and to get there bleak and waterless deserts had to be crossed, some infested by fierce reptiles and boiling streams. When the soul set out on his journey, he took with him a stave to fight off unwanted entities and food for nourishment. His initial challenge was to climb the western mountains and then enter the Kingdom of the Dead. As he neared his destination a large sycamore tree stood before him; on this, clusters of fruit were visible among its succulent foliage. As he approached it, a goddess leaned down from the tree trunk, displaying only the upper part of her body. In her hands she held a plate heaped with cake and fruit and a pot of clear fresh water. To continue the journey, the soul must eat and drink the magic offerings so as to become a servant of the gods. If he rejected the hospitality of the tree goddess, he would return to the dark and miserable tomb from which he came, and forever lead there a solitary and joyless existence.

The soul who accepted the hospitality could proceed on its journey, encountering further more sinister and dangerous trials, as evil spirits and demons sought to defeat him, so he would suffer a second death which would cause him to cease to exist in any form. He battled with a gigantic tortoise using his stave to defeat it, elsewhere serpents lurked and were poised to strike. These too were enemies to be overcome. Insects with poisonous stings attacked him. Without doubt, the soul's most formidable enemy was Seth, the murderer of Osiris. He was the terror of the good god and men, who appeared as a huge red monster bearing a head like a camel, with the body of a hound, his long forked tail erect and venomous, desperate to devour the pilgrim. When the evil Seth has been overcome and driven back, the soul progresses until he reaches the bank of a wide river. There a magic boat awaited, its crew silent divinities that neither offer nor provide any assistance. Before he could embark, he had to answer each question asked of him by the boat, and relate how it is constructed in every part. If the papyrus roll that was laid beside his mummy contained the secret of the boat and the magic formulae, that too must be repeated. Only then could he be ferried across the river and taken to the Kingdom of Osiris.

The dark and sinister ferryman was called *Turnface,* and his face constantly looked in the opposite direction from the dead who called to him. After climbing on board the boat, the soul's journey was still nowhere near its end. The soul wished greatly to be among the happy beings who already had their dwellings in the blessed fields of Aalu, but first the soul had to be tried by Osiris, the King of the Dead and the Judge of All. The solitary approach to paradise was through the Hall of Justice which slowly rose before him, unwelcoming, dark and mysterious. The gate was shut fast and no mortal man could draw the securing bolts or enter without the permission of Osiris. The soul now stood before the gate with both his hands held high in adoration of the great king, who beheld him from within the Hall of Justice. Then, in clear, full voice the soul proclaimed its negative confession before Osiris:

Hail, unto you, O great God, you who are lord of the truth! Lo! I draw nigh to thee now, O my lord, and my eyes behold your beauty. You I know, and I know also the two-and-forty gods assembled with you in the hall of justice; They observe all the deeds of the wicked; They devour those who seek to do evil; They drink the blood of those who are condemned before you, O just and good king. Hail! Lord of Justice; you I know, I come before you even now to speak what is true; I will not utter what is false, O Lord of All.

The soul then recited the ritual Negative Confession in which he claimed to be guiltless of the offences that are punishable:

I have not committed crimes against people. I have not mistreated the cattle. I have not sinned in the place of truth (temple or necropolis). I have not known that which should not be known. I have not done any harm. I have not exacted more than was my due. I have not committed blasphemy against the gods. I have not robbed the poor. I have not done what the gods hate. I have not spoken ill of a servant to their master. I have not caused pain. I have not caused tears. I have not killed or ordered anyone to kill.
I have not caused suffering.
I have not damaged the temple offerings.
I have not stolen bread from the gods.

I have not stolen bread from the dead.
I have not committed adultery nor defiled myself.
I have not taken milk from children's mouths.
I have not neglected the time of meat offerings.
I have not stopped a god in procession.
I have done no evil against any man.
I have never caused my kinsfolk to be put to death.
I have not caused false witnesses to speak in the hall of justice.
I have not done that which is hated by the gods.
I am not a worker of wickedness.
I have never oppressed a servant with too much work.
I have not caused men to hunger nor to weep.
I have not been devoid of good works, nor have I acted weakly or with meanness.
I am not a murderer.
I have not conspired to have another put to death.
I have not plotted to make another grieve.
I have not taken away temple offerings.
I have not stinted the food offered to the gods.
I have not despoiled the dead.
I have never committed adultery.
I have not failed to keep myself pure as a priest.
I have not lessened the corn measure.
I have not shortened the hand measure.
I have not tampered with the balance.
I have not deprived children of milk.
I have not stolen cattle from the meadows.
I have not snared the birds consecrated to the gods.
I have not taken fish from holy lakes.
I have not prevented (Nile) waters from a channel.
I have not turned aside the water.
I have not stolen water from a channel.
I have not put out the fire when it should burn.
I have never kept from the Nine Gods what was their due.
I have not prevented the temple cattle from grazing on my land.
I have not obstructed a god (his image) when he came forth (in a festival procession).

I am pure! I am pure! I am pure! I am pure!
I am pure as the great heron of Hnes.
No harm shall befall me in this Hall of two truths,
for I know the name of all the gods within it,
all the followers of the great god (Osiris):
O Wide-Strider of Heliopolis, I have not done evil;
O Flame-Embracer of Khehara, I have not committed robbery;
O Beaky of Khmun, I am not guilty of greed;
O Shadow-Eater from the Cave, I am not guilty of stealing;
O Terrifying Face of Rostau, I am not guilty of murder;
O Wrecker from Huy, I am not guilty of winking;
O Backward Face of the Pit, I am not guilty of homosexuality.
Hail to you gods!
I know you and know your names,
I shall not fall down in fear of you,
you shall not accuse me of a crime.

The jackal-headed god Anubis then strode forward from the hall and led the soul by the hand to be taken before Osiris, who had already listened to the Negative Confession and now sat in silence. Not a word would be uttered as the soul entered the Hall of Two-Truths (Hall of Judgment). Osiris, the King of the Dead was enthroned on his dais. His crown rested upon his head, in one hand he held a crook and in the other a flail. Before him stood the balance on which the mortal heart of the dead man would be weighed. Thoth, the recording god, stood next to the balance, and both Horus and Maat, goddess of truth and justice were present. Below sat a guardian of the balance, in the form of a monster called Ammut (the Devourer), a creature with the head of a crocodile, the body of a lion and the hind legs of a hippopotamus, which was ready to fall upon condemned sinners standing before the great god Osiris.

Around the hall lay in wait the forty-two animal gods known as the Assessors, the judges of the dead. Bearing names such as Beaky, or Shadow-Eater, they were ready to tear the wicked and condemned to pieces. The soul watched the gods deliberately weighing his heart in the balance, while the symbol of Maat, an ostrich feather, occupied the opposite scale. The soul cried out to his heart not to witness against him. 'O heart that was mine do not say "Behold the things he has done." Permit me not to be wronged in the presence of the great god.' If the heart was found to be neither too heavy nor too light, the dead man was acquitted. Thoth stepped forward and made known the result of the weighing to Osiris, who in turn instructed that the heart be restored to the man on trial. *'He has won the victory,'* the King of the Dead exclaimed. *'Now let him dwell with the spirits and the gods in the fields of Aalu he is true of voice.'* The deceased was then taken by Horus to stand before Osiris and told to *'throw away your mask and undo your wrappings!'*

The divine Kingdom was a greater, more glorious Egypt in which the souls resided, a place where each and every man was allotted a task and the journey was complete. When the soul wished to return to visit familiar scenes on earth, it entered the body of a bird or an animal, or blossomed as a flower. It might also visit the tomb as the *ka* and reanimate the mummy, then go forth to gaze on scenes that were familiar in other days. The souls of the dead men whom Osiris condemned because of their sins committed on earth, were subjected to excruciating torture, pain and suffering. They were already aware that *'wrongdoers shall not behold the face of god'* and that hearts that were overweight with sin were thrown to Ammut and the Assessors.

One might say that was a fate worse than death.

Chapter 8

The Curse of the Pharaohs

It is estimated that for over 500 years the pharaohs of ancient Egypt arranged for their tombs to be built within the hills across the Nile from Thebes (now Luxor), a site now known as the Valley of the Kings. The tombs and the valley remained relatively untouched for centuries, although Roman graffiti indicates that the tombs were frequently visited. One of the first modern treasure-seekers to dig in the valley was ex-circus strongman Giovanni Belzoni. In 1817, after digging for around ten days, he came upon three unknown tombs including that of King Seti I. He later published his memoirs, describing the uncovering of the tombs and how a battering ram was used to open ancient sealed doorways, whereupon he found 'heaps of mummies in all directions. I sunk altogether among the broken mummies, with a crash of bones, rags and wooden cases.' Belzoni's find inspired a host of tomb robbers to visit the valley and loot whatever treasures they could find. Belzoni himself died in suspicious surroundings in 1823, after contracting a mysterious disease that was thought have come from the excavations of the tomb of Seti I.

By 1827 twenty-one ancient burial tombs had been located in the valley, resulting in mass grave robbery and a black market for antiquities. By the middle of the nineteenth century, tourists were regular visitors to the valley, where they would be offered genuine artifacts removed from the tombs. It wasn't until 1857 that the Egyptian government felt it necessary to establish the Antiquities Service and create a museum where items recovered from the tombs could be displayed and stored securely.

Later, in 1858, incidents of strange deaths relating to the ancient Egyptians began to be reported. It is said that four fit and healthy

European tourists, who had visited the pyramids at Giza, died suddenly and within days of one another. The deaths were officially recorded as the effects of various fevers caught in the Egyptian desert. It has been suggested that the physicians who carried out autopsy examinations of the corpses later testified that the report was fraudulent and their original findings had been edited. They were convinced that there was no known medical explanation or reason for the untimely deaths.

By 1902, around forty tombs had been found in the valley. In 2015, over sixty tombs are known to exist in the Valley of the Kings, from small tombs which could be described as holes in the ground to much larger tombs. Most of them held little evidence of any defined curse ascribed to them. That, however, does not mean to say that tomb curses did not exist: they did, and we have a wealth of clear evidence supporting this fact. Robbery and theft from the tombs was a serious issue, so pharaohs requested that their bespoke tomb designers employ unique and ingenious means to prevent and deter robbers from desecrating the tombs. Many of the tombs discovered displayed evidence of traps deliberately set to prevent unauthorised access into the valuable inner confines, and some bore hieroglyphic inscriptions on sealed outer doors that were believed to be curses making all kinds of threats, seemingly with no moral boundaries. The phrasing and location of the tomb inscription was meant to strike terror into the heart of any potential tomb raider. One curse that seems to cover all eventualities comes from the administrator of the 18th dynasty, Amenhotep, the son of Hapu. He threatens anyone who would damage his tomb with a comprehensive list of punishments. They would:

Lose their earthly positions and honors, be incinerated in a furnace in execration rites, capsize and drown at sea, have no successors, receive no tomb or funerary offerings of their own, and their bodies would decay because they will starve without sustenance and their bones will perish.

Another well-known curse is preserved in the Dynasty 5 Pyramid Texts (Utterance 534, §1278-9):

As for anyone who shall lay a finger on this pyramid and this temple which belong to me and my ka, he will have laid his finger on the Mansion of Horus in the firmament, he will have offended the Lady of the Mansion... his affair will be judged by the Ennead and he will be nowhere and his house will be nowhere; he will be one proscribed, one who eats himself.

The vast majority of the royal tombs did not have curses, but threatening inscriptions have been found in many private tombs, generally those dating back to the Old Kingdom. These effectively consist of the tomb owner invoking judgment in the underworld on any would-be tomb violator. The following inscription was found on an Anubis shrine: 'It is I who hinder the sand from choking the secret chamber. I am for the protection of the deceased'. Such messages depict Anubis as a protector of the dead, an entity that possesses mystical power and the ability to move between the mortal and spiritual world. Another inscription was found in the tomb of Meni, a courtier of the Fourth Dynasty:

As for any man who did these things for me, he should not be dissatisfied, because, whether sculptor or stonemason, I paid him for it. Let the crocodile be against him in the water, the snake against him on the land. I have never done anything against him and it is the god who will judge him for it.

The following curses/threats have been found in tombs. Where it has been possible to identify a tomb bearing such inscriptions, these are detailed in brackets. The mortuary temple built in honour of Amenhotep was protected by the following curse:

As for anyone who will come after me and who will find the foundation of the funerary tomb in destruction... as for anyone who will take the personnel from among my people... as for all others who will turn them astray... I will not allow them to perform their scribal function... I will put them in the furnace of the King... His uraeus will vomit flame upon the top of their heads, demolishing their flesh and devouring their bones. They will become Apophis (a divine serpent who is vanquished) on the morning of the day of the year. They will capsize in the sea which will devour their bodies. They will not receive honours received by virtuous people. They will not be able to swallow offerings from the dead. One will not pour them water in libation... Their sons will not occupy their places, their women will be violated before their eyes. Their great ones will be so lost in their houses that they will be upon the floor... They will not understand the words of the King at the time when he is in joy. They will be doomed to the knife on the day of the massacre... Their bodies will decay because they will starve and will not have sustenance and their bones will perish. As for anything you shall do against this my grave the like shall be done against yours. Every man who shall interfere with this my stela, I will be judged with him in the place where judgment is made. As for any man who will make a disturbance, I shall be judged with him. A crocodile be against him in the water; a snake be against him on land, he who would do anything against this tomb. Never did I do a thing against him. It is the god who will judge. As for anybody who shall enter this tomb in his impurity: I shall ring his neck as a bird's.

Inscription found in tomb of High Priest Hermeru, Dyn. 5:
As for any man who shall destroy these, it is the god Thoth who shall destroy him. As for him who shall destroy this inscription: He shall not reach his home. He shall not embrace his children. He shall not see success. As for anything that you might do against this tomb of mine of the West, the like shall be done against your property. I am an excellent lector priest, exceeding knowledgeable in secret spells and all magic. As for any person who will enter into this tomb of mine in their impurity, having eaten the abominations that excellent akh-spirits abominate, or who do not purify themselves as they should purify themselves for an excellent akh who does what his lord praises, I shall seize him like a goose (wring his neck), placing fear in him at seeing ghosts upon earth, that they might be fearful of an excellent akh... But as for anyone who will enter into this tomb of mine being pure and peaceful regarding it, I shall be his protective

backer in the West in the court of the great god. Found in tomb of Ankhmahor - Saqqara - Old Kindom.

I shall seize his neck like that of a goose. Inscription of Hermeru, Dynasty 6.

He shall die from hunger and thirst. Found on a statue of Herihor, High Priest of Amun, Dyn. 20-21.

He shall have no heir. Inscription of Tuthmosis I, Dyn. 18.

His years shall be diminished. Found on a statue of Monthuemhat, Dyn. 25-26.

His lifetime shall not exist on earth. Inscribed on the tomb of Senmut, Dyn. 18.

His estate shall belong to the fire, and his house shall belong to the consuming flame ... His relatives shall detest him. Found on the tomb of Tefib, Dyn. 9-10.

He shall be miserable and persecuted. Inscribed on the tomb of Penniut, Dyn. 20.

His office shall be taken away before his face and it shall be given to a man who is his enemy. Found on a statue of the scribe Amenhotep, Dyn. 18.

His face shall be spat at. Found on El-Hasaia tomb, Dyn. 26.

A donkey (the animal of Seth) shall violate him, a donkey shall violate his wife. Deir el-Bahri Graffito No.11, Dyn. 20.

His heart shall not be content in life. Found on a statue of Wersu, Dyn. 18.

He shall be cooked together with the condemned. Found on the tomb of Khety II, Dyn. 9-10.

His name shall not exist in the land of Egypt. Found on a statue of the high priest Herihor, Dyn. 20-21.

Listen all of you! The priest of Hathor will beat twice any of you who enters this tomb or does harm to it. The gods will confront him because I am honored by his Lord. The gods will not allow anything to happen to me. Anyone who does anything bad to my tomb, then the crocodile, hippopotamus, and lion will eat him. Inscription found in the entrance to the Dynasty 3 tomb of Petety at Giza.

He shall not exist. Found on the tomb of Khnumhotep, Dyn. 12.

His wife shall be taken away before his face. Apanage Stele, Dyn. 22.

His years shall be diminished. Found on a statue of Monthuemhat, Dyn. 25-26.

The curse upon the offerings to Sarenput I, nomarch of Elephantine under Senusret I (Dynasty 12), read:

As for every mayor, every wab-priest, every scribe and every nobleman who shall take [the offering] from the statue, his arm shall be cut off like that of this bull, his neck shall be twisted off like that of a bird, his office shall not exist, the position of his son shall not exist, his house shall not exist in Nubia, his tomb shall not exist in the necropolis, his god shall not accept his white bread, his flesh shall belong to the fire, his children shall belong to the fire, his corpse shall not be to the ground, I shall be against him as a crocodile on the water, as a serpent on earth, and as an enemy in the necropolis.

Another curse is clear in its purpose:

He who trespasses upon my property or who shall injure my tomb or drag out my mummy, the sun god shall punish him. He shall not bequeath his goods to his children; his heart shall not have pleasure in life; he shall not receive water in the tomb; and his soul shall be destroyed forever. As to anyone who violates my body which is in the tomb and who shall remove my image from tomb, he shall be hateful to the gods, and he shall not receive water on the altar of Osiris. (Found in the tomb of Ursa)

Some tombs ask for prayers, with the deceased owner promising to assist the living if they will say the offering prayer for the dead. The explorer Harkhuf is typical:

Oh you living people, who are upon the earth, [who shall pass by this tomb] going downstream or going upstream, say: 'A thousand loaves [of bread] and thousand jars of beer for the owner of this tomb;' I will [do good] for their sakes in the

Underworld. I am an excellent, well equipped spirit, a ritual priest, whose mouth knows [powerful spells].

Harkhuf's threat, or curse, is typical as well: 'As for any man who shall enter into [this] tomb, ... [I will seize] him like a wild fowl; he shall be judged by the great god.' These curses basically consist of the owner of the tomb invoking judgment in the underworld on any would-be violators. The inscription served as a reminder that the ancient Egyptians' responsibility was to Maat, which is best described as the complete system of order and justice, the overall pattern of life, and reiterated the potential dire consequences of any kind of rebellious action against Maat. It remains, potentially, the most powerful message to travel the passage of time, as subsequent races and religions since have inherited a fear and respect of the curse of the pharaoh. In some instances important decrees were protected by means of threat, as the following example shows:

As to any King and powerful person who will forgive him, he will not receive the white crown, he will not raise up the red crown, he will dwell upon the throne of Horus of the living. As for any commander or mayor who will petition my Lord to pardon him, his property and his fields will be put as offerings for my father Min of Coptos.

It wasn't only tombs that bore such curses, they appeared in letters too. A letter written in the Middle Kingdom from one woman to another closed with 'May you be sick when you read this.' In another, a woman who had adopted servants as her children and wished to assure their position wrote:

As Amun endures and the ruler endures, I make the people whom I have recorded freshmen of the land of Pharaoh. Should a son of a daughter or a brother or a sister of their mother or their father contest with them – except for this son of mine, Pendiu – for they are no longer slaves to him, but are brothers and sisters to him, being freemen of the land – may a donkey copulate with him and a female donkey copulate with his wife, if anyone shall call one of them a slave.

The evidence for the pharaoh's mysterious curse causing hurt or physical harm to anyone remains purely anecdotal. That is, the evidence consists entirely of stories of deaths, illnesses, and disasters that have befallen those who have worked on the pyramids or, in some instances, have visited them or touched genuine artifacts. To date, despite valiant efforts by scribes, writers, journalists, film producers and documentary film makers, no hard evidence has been produced to show that the countless tragic and seemingly mysterious events that are associated with ancient Egypt and the pyramids can be classed matters of coincidence, gross exaggeration, over indulgence of the imagination, or if they are actually in some way connected to the ancient pharaohs.

I believe that, like the ancient Egyptians, we as a civilisation like to think and believe there is an afterlife, a place where we could all exist in peace and tranquility. Today, we still have embalmers and burial rituals and ceremonies for individual religions, we still put personalised inscriptions on tombs and graves, and we have psychics, mediums, ghost-hunters all with huge followings – who want us to believe they are in contact with the 'other world'. Perhaps worst of all, we still have tomb and grave robbers. As a modern race, have we really progressed?

Chapter 9

Tutankhamun's Tomb – The Hidden Story

We have previously discussed the curious deaths associated with the opening of King Tutankhamun's tomb. Primarily, we are reliant upon the testimony of the lead archaeologist, Howard Carter, but over the years Carter's credibility has come into question.

Lord Carnarvon was the first to allegedly fall victim to the curse, followed some time later, curiously in the same hotel, by the American Egyptologist Arthur Meiss. Shortly thereafter, a number of other scientists were found dead, including Archibald Douglas Reid, a professor of radiology. Reid was the first to lift the linen fabrics from the mummy, and to reveal the body of Tutankhamen for X-ray photography. Between 1922 and 1929, more than thirteen Egyptologists died. Each of them had a connection to the tomb of Tutankhamun, either the opening of it, or having worked in it or on the associated artifacts. However, the lead archaeologist Howard Carter declared that no curse existed, and none was ever found in the pharaoh's tomb. He reportedly dismissed the idea as nonsense, and attributed the deaths to a strange set of coincidences. He also used himself as an example, because he lived on long after discovering the tomb and working in it. That might have been the end of the matter, but there are many who question the integrity of Howard Carter. Some even accuse him of deliberate lies about entering and examining of the tomb.

The curse was enthusiastically reported in the press, with numerous versions of the alleged curse appearing. However, the first people to discuss it, some of the Egyptian tomb workers, disclosed that a curse tablet was found at the tomb, which read: 'Death Shall Come on Swift Wings To He Who Disturbs The Peace of The King'. As with so many matters, Carter swore each of the tomb workers to absolute secrecy about anything and everything that was taking place at the dig site. The world's press were in Luxor in their hundreds covering the find; each reporter was desperate for a story and therefore doing their utmost to find one. The tomb workers were not foolish enough to speak with the press; instead they kept their own counsel and only spoke of the excavations and treasures to those closest to them. These are stories that have been passed down through generations before reaching this book.

There remains a belief among some Egyptians that a curse tablet was found on the door of the tomb, but it was removed by Carter because he knew it would cause panic among his workforce, who would refuse to enter the tomb and therefore hinder the excavations. So Carter allegedly destroyed the tablet, smashing into pieces until it was dust, and threatened the tomb workers, forcing them into silence. It was effectively one of the first 'media blackouts' on record.

Historians, archaeologists and mainstream scientists have little time for anecdotal evidence, particularly as it questions the absolute integrity of one of their own – Howard Carter. The official story has Carter identifying the sealed tomb door on 5 November and, by his own account, he felt 'almost overwhelmed' by the urge to break open the irksome door, but he resisted and buried the stairs once again. The following day he sent a telegram to Carnarvon, advising him of the find and summoning him to the dig site. Carter then waited for over two weeks for Carnarvon to arrive to officially break in and enter the tomb, which showed signs of a previous ancient break in and tomb robbery.

How much of this official version is true? We can assess it based on the facts that we have. In 1947 one of Carter's team, the highly respected Manchester-born chemist Alfred Lucas, who worked for the Egyptian Antiquities Service from 1923-1932 and with Carter for nine dig seasons, spoke out and sowed the seed of doubt about the truth behind the entering of the tomb. It should be said that Lucas had nothing to gain from the details he offered; if anything it would cast doubt on his own reputation.

Lucas stated, in a Cairo-based scientific journal, that he knew that Carter had secretly broken open the door to the burial chamber and entered. A few hours later he resealed it with a different (authentic-looking) antique seal. Is it really feasible that Carter, on the brink of such a fantastic find, could resist the temptation to enter and have a look around, and remove some objects for his own private purposes? Carter was, at that time, hardly respected in his field; he had consistently upset officials and had an overly, some say unjustified, high opinion of himself.

Carter claimed that the tomb robbers had stolen perfumes, cosmetics and linen, and that a later break in was more destructive and had damaged many artifacts and treasures. The question remains, would genuine tomb robbers really concentrate on stealing perfumes and cosmetics, and ignore the wealth of gold treasure, rings and jewellery that lay all around the tomb? In addition, in Carter's own words, 'in the ante-chamber there had been some sort of attempt to clear up after the plunderer's visit.' Would a tomb robber seriously try to clear up the mess he had made prior to exiting the tomb? Carter continues to discuss the damage to the second chamber door; 'a small breach had been made near the bottom, just wide enough to admit a boy or a slightly built man, and that the hole made had subsequently been filled up and resealed.' The space within the chambers was limited, perhaps sufficient for one individual to clamber through and forage through the riches on display, then extract himself armed with the stolen goods. At the time of burial, the tomb was sealed and access blocked by mounds of rubble, yet Carter would have us believe that robbers removed this debris to create sufficient space to reseal the point of entry and disguise their break in? Such effort on behalf of the robbers must be regarded as highly speculative and most improbable. Bearing in mind that the tomb robbers would be acting quickly, and that breaking in would take a good deal of effort (removing sufficient debris from the blocked up passageway to allow minimal access to the door), once the tomb had been accessed and plundered they would have achieved their purpose but the risk element would have increased. With incriminating stolen property in their possession, being caught might mean instant death. They would waste no time fleeing the scene.

To further support the claim of Alfred Lucas, we have the 1979 revelations of Thomas Hoving, Director of the Metropolitan Museum of Art (1967–77) who published an account apparently penned by Lord Carnarvon shortly before his death. This claimed that Howard Carter, Carnarvon himself, and his daughter Lady Evelyn Herbert and entered the tomb at night. They had got through two sealed doors and into the burial chamber. Entry had been gained by breaking a small hole in the bottom of the door to the burial chamber; on leaving, the hole was covered with reeds. There is evidence that Carter was purloining artifacts and either selling or giving them away: indeed, he was caught in the act by Pierre Lacau, who was then Egypt's Director of Antiquities. Lacau, accompanied by some of his staff and in the absence of Howard Carter, visited the tomb on 29 March to check progress and look at the inventories. He was pleased to note that Carter was maintaining accurate logs of everything discovered in the tomb with a unique triple index system: items were recorded in the official register, on the box in which they were stored and items themselves were labelled.

All seemed well until Lacau went into one of the side chambers of the tomb and saw a stack of Fortnum and Mason champagne crates. All of them, with the exception of one, were open. The closed and sealed box bore a label that simply stated 'red wine'. Lacau was suspicious and instructed his staff to force the crate open. When they did they were stunned to find not red wine, but, wrapped in surgical gauze, a wooden bust of the head of Tutankhamun. The image portrayed the Egyptian god-king rising from a lotus flower. The statue was in the unique 'Amarna' style of art, first developed by Akhenaten, with the back of the head exaggeratedly long. Artistically and historically it was a major find within the tomb, so why was it not registered anywhere, and more to the point, why was it in a box marked 'red wine'? The Egyptian party recognised that something was wrong and immediately took possession of the bust. Carter later claimed the bust had been found in the passageway leading into the tomb, and he had not got round to documenting its existence in the official register. It should also be noted that Carter fails to mention the existence of the bust in the first volume of his 1923 book, *The Tomb of Tutankhamun*. Something so overtly valuable and he omits it from all records! One can only be suspicious, particularly as Carter was apparently meticulous in the recording detail of artifacts found in the tomb.

Subsequently, a variety of treasures that can only have come from the tomb have been unearthed and are on display in museums across the globe. Some bear the royal inscription of Tutankhamun and are clearly from the tomb, yet none appear in the official register! It is believed that up to 60 per cent of the contents of Tutankhamun's tomb were never registered, or recorded. Carter claims this is because they had been stolen by tomb robbers, again deflecting any blame or doubt about his own involvement. Can we believe that objects were being randomly stolen by others without his knowledge, when he was so precious and controlling about managing every aspect of recovery of the treasures removed from the tomb?

It has long been my belief that Howard Carter told his own version of what happened. It must be regarded as the 'official' version, and while I am not a believer in conspiracy theories, I do believe the truth of what happened in the tomb of the boy King Tutankhamun has been suppressed because of the scandal that would ensure if the truth was ever revealed. I don't believe that Carnarvon knew the scale of the pilfering; Carter was probably acting alone in this respect. Carnarvon was being guided by his archaeologist and so trusted his judgement on all matters relating to the legalities of the excavations. There can be no doubt that the fame this find created benefited Carter; he was awarded an honorary doctorate and rubbed shoulders with many eminent and powerful authorities, including United States President Calvin Coolidge, who invited him to tea! Horst Beinlich, Egyptologist at Wurzburg University, described Carter as a 'thoroughly honest man full of idealism.' It is only now that we can question the accuracy of this opinion, in the light of evidence that suggests that Howard Carter, for so long a great hero of the British Empire, manipulated the discovery for his own benefit. Many of Howard Carter's peers suspected him to be stealing artifacts from the tomb and knew of the deceit. On 25 January 1923, his friend and fellow Egyptologist Arthur Weigall wrote a letter to Carter. The following is an extract:

The situation is this. You and Carnarvon made the initial error when you discovered the tomb of thinking that the old British prestige in this country is still maintained and that you could do more or less what you liked. You have found this tomb, however, at a moment when the last spark may send the whole magazine sky-high, when the utmost diplomacy is needed, when Egyptians have to be considered in a way which you and I are not accustomed to, and when the slightest false step may do the utmost disservice to our own enemy. You opened the tomb before you notified the Government representative, and the natives all say that you may therefore have had the opportunity of stealing some of the millions' of pounds of gold of which you talked. (I give this as an instance of native gossip about you).

Carter did not respond in writing to this communication, but he did so in kind, in a manner that he knew would greatly upset Weigall. He refused to allow Weigall any private access to the tomb and he was only able to visit it as a member of the public. Carter later wrote of the matter 'Much to his chagrin he was not allowed in the tomb except with the public'. If this was a modern-day police investigation Carter would have many questions to answer, particularly concerning the initial entering of the tomb and the finding of the wooden bust found by Pierre Lacau. Can we truly trust Carter's version as accurate and truthful? If the answer is not a resounding yes, which I do not believe it can be, then we must question everything. The finding of the tomb of King Tutankhamun was not only Carter's crowning moment, it was also viewed as a wonderful achievement by the British Empire. The thought that the find was potentially tainted by deception is not palatable at all. Was there a curse in Tutankhamun's tomb? We will never know. Carter destroyed much during his excavation of that tomb, not least the mummified body of the pharaoh himself. To my mind there is a real possibility that he intentionally destroyed things that might have hindered or negatively affected him, and prevented him from reaching his professional goals.

Finally, evidence exists that Carter, or someone in his team, plundered much of the treasure. Artifacts that can only have come from the tomb have turned up in museums across the world. In the Louvre in Paris there is a 'ushabti' figure bearing Tutankhamun's inscription;

in Kansas City (United States) two golden hawks' heads, which had been taken from the necklace laid next to the mummy's skin, are on display. None of these are registered in Carter's tomb records.

Howard Carter was rightly recognised for his work discovering the tomb. However, I believe that temptation got the better of him; he entered the tomb illegally, stole objects and fraudulently recorded details and manipulated photographic evidence of the find. The seeming web of lies and deceit, which is only now gradually being uncovered, casts a shadow over the excellent work he carried out. I am certain that the greatest archaeological find of all time has been seriously tainted by his deception.

Chapter 10

Mysterious Happenings

We have already made mention of Egyptologist Arthur Weigall. Weigall, who was a firm believer in the curse, was involved in another inexplicable incident. On a visit to Egypt with his wife and an American artist friend, Joseph Lindon Smith, who was also accompanied by his wife, the group decided, as a light-hearted piece of entertainment, to act out a play at the head of the Valley of the Queens, in front of a selected audience. At one of the rehearsals, however, Mrs Smith was suddenly struck with a constant fierce pain in her eyes. Later the same day Mrs Weigall fell ill and developed severe abdominal pains. Both women were rushed to hospital. The medical teams could find no reason for the pains, but advised both women to rest. Local people soon began talking of the curse, and Weigall immediately cancelled the play, believing that the spirits of the goddesses buried within the Valley of the Queens had somehow attacked both women, causing them to fall ill as a warning. Weigall later said of the incident: 'I have heard the most absurd nonsense talked in Egypt by those who believe in the malevolence of the ancient dead; but at the same time I try to keep an open mind on the subject.' In the temple of Ptah at Karnak stands a statue of Sekmhet. This statue has a terrible reputation and is reputed to be cursed. For many years it has been thought that on moonlit nights the statue wanders the local streets seeking out children to seize and kill. Reports of child disappearances seem to have haunted the region. It seems incredible that no one believed there to be some kind of child abductor operating within their midst, nor a serial killer, and that the incidents were blamed on the soul of Sekhmet.

Sekhmet was an aggressive solar goddess, believed to be the

instrument of divine retribution. She is depicted with the body of a human and a leonine head, often surmounted by a sun disk. According to the legend, death first came into the world when the Eye of Ra was sent down as Sekhmet to punish rebellious humanity. 'She who dances on blood' almost destroyed the entire human race before she was tricked into stopping. Since humans were believed to have sprung from the tears of the Eye of Ra, Sekhmet was slaughtering her own children. Of all the archer goddesses in Egypt, Sekhmet was the most feared: her arrows were said to transform into seven messengers who inflicted pain, torture, plague and destruction upon humanity. At one time, local villagers were so irate and fearful about the statue, that they grouped together, entered the temple and physically attacked it with clubs and stones. No matter how hard they tried, they could not destroy it.

Over the years, there have been reports of visitors to the temple claiming that they have seen the statue move. Several have reportedly become hysterical and been carried away from the area to calm down. Mary Nicholson was one of a number of people who were looking at the statue when several people said they heard a strange creaking noise:

We stood looking at it, the statue of Sekhmet, nobody had told us anything untoward about it, and we had no idea at the time of its fearsome reputation, it was just another amazing statue. I would think there were about five of us looking at it when we heard this grinding creaking sound coming from within the monument. We all took a step back fearing an earthquake and that it might fall forward. The noise continued for a few more seconds, and by now we all had our eyes transfixed on the statue. Then it moved, just slightly initially, but I definitely saw its head move. Then its arm extended out towards us, right where we stood, in its hand it is holding a lotus blossom. The arm appeared to extend forward, moving closer to us, and as it did so its head moved. It was one of those occasions when you think someone is playing a practical joke on you, but you aren't certain. We all laughed nervously, and then it moved again, this time we screamed out in terror. One woman was screaming 'It's alive, it's alive!' Two officials came over to us and asked what had happened, so we told them, expecting them to dismiss our claims. They didn't. Instead, they asked us to leave the shrine area where the statue stood, and to join other groups of tourists. One of the men told us that the statue was cursed and that many people had seen it move, even local Egyptian people. They wouldn't allow us to take a photograph of it once this happened, we just had to get out of the area. When we spoke to other Egyptian people about it, people in the museums, they said they were aware of many similar reports and that it was a belief that the statue of Sekhmet was cursed by an evil soul. I tried to forget the entire episode but I still have nightmares about it and the most concerning thing is, I can't explain it at all. No one can, but it moved, I swear it did.

A further unconnected mysterious happening occurred on 10 March 1971, this time not at Karnak, but in Sakkara, on the edge of the desert approximately 20 miles south of Cairo. Men working on a dig had been labouring in the desert sun since 7am. It was 2pm when they downed tools and stopped for the day, exhausted after bringing tons of rubble and rock to the surface from 30 feet down. Sakkara had become an attractive place to dig; the cemetery has been identified as Memphis, ancient city of the dead, and stretches some 4½ miles in length and 500 to 1,500 yards wide.

Having discovered a hidden tomb in Sakkara, Walter Brian Emery, professor of Egyptology, took ill and later died. The circumstances are as follows. One of the workers in his team uncovered a deep hole that contained a statue, not more than 20cm in length. It was a statue of Osiris, the God of Dead. The worker immediately handed the statue over to Emery, who took it with him to his dig-house. There he placed it on a table and took a shower, while his assistant Ali-al Khouli went to sit on the outside terrace. Suddenly the assistant heard a noise from inside the house. Thinking it was Emery, he called out to him but received no answer. In search of Emery, he opened the door to the bathroom. The assistant later reported:

I sat here on the couch. Suddenly I heard moaning coming from the washroom. I looked through the door, which was ajar, and

*saw Emery holding onto the basin. 'Are you sick?' I called out,
but the professor did not reply. He stood there as if paralyzed. I
grabbed him by the shoulders and dragged him onto the couch.
Then I ran for the telephone.*

An ambulance was called and Emery was rushed to the British hospital
in Cairo. The diagnosis was clear; paralysis of the right side. The
unfortunate Emery was unable to speak and was comforted at his
bedside by Mary, his wife, who accompanied him on countless
expeditions. Mary remained at his side throughout the night, but the
next day, Thursday 11 March 1971, Walter Bryan Emery died. The
Cairo newspaper *Al Ahram* reported his death, writing: 'This strange
occurrence leads us to believe that the legendary curse of the pharaohs
has been reactivated.'

A similar fate befell German archaeologist Karl Richard Lepsius
(1810–84). After receiving his doctorate following his dissertation, *De
tabulis Eugubinis,* in 1833, he travelled to Paris and attended lectures
by French classicist Jean Letronne, an early disciple of Jean-François
Champollion and his work on the decipherment of the Egyptian
language. Lepsius had successfully carried out a dig in Valley of the
Kings and was fortunate to discover a complete tomb. When he left,
he took with him an entire pillar from the tomb of Seth I, which was
transported to Berlin. There, he suddenly fell ill and was paralysed
down one side of his body. Much later, he was diagnosed as suffering
from cancer. He is said to have believed his paralysis was put upon
him by the wrath of the pharaohs, who were angered by his actions.

Another German-born doctor and Egyptologist to suffer was
Theodoor Bilharz, who first came to Egypt with Professor William
Greznera, and worked with the king of Egypt, Khedive Ismaïl. In 1850
Greznera left the country to make his way back to Germany, leaving
Bilharz to stay on alone. Bilharz went in search of undiscovered
monuments and relics of the ancient Egyptian era and investigated the
anatomy of many mummies. In 1856, he was elected President of the
Anatomy and Pathology Department at the University of Freiburg. In
the same year he discovered the eggs of the bilharzia worm in the body
of an Egyptian mummy from the 20th dynasty. In 1858 he became
head of the Egyptian Researchers and Archaeologists' Association, and

in 1862 he travelled with Ernest II's wife during her journey to Luxor. It was during his return trip to Cairo that he suffered an asthma attack and passed out. Two weeks later, he died aged just 37, having been in a deep coma since the day of the attack. The solitary reason given for his death was the mysteriously sudden asthma attack! Some believe his death was connected with a curse, because of the desecration of hundreds of mummies he had examined as part of his studies.

One of the most curious incidents connected to ancient Egyptian archaeology is the deaths of Sir William Matthew Flinders Petrie and his American colleague, Professor George Reisner, in 1942. Both were prominent Egyptologists. Reisner had previously discovered the tomb of Khufu's mother, and he made media history when he shared his knowledge of the Great Pyramid by delivering a worldwide broadcast from within the King's Chamber in 1939. In the spring of 1942, Reisner was working inside the pyramid when he collapsed. Although he was almost entirely blind, he was articulate and extremely vocal and he had made no comment about feeling unwell. The onset of the illness was sudden, and resulted in him being dragged from the pyramid paralysed. Shortly afterwards he died. The cause of his death remains the subject of speculation. Reisner was buried in the American cemetery in Mari Girgis, Cairo.

Catastrophe struck again on 28 July of the same year, when Petrie was making his way home to England. While in Jerusalem, he too suddenly and inexplicably died. Stories of the curse quickly circulated and were instantly dismissed by mainstream historians and academics.

Are curses a thing of the past? As recently as 1992 a team of archaeologists excavating some of the smaller tombs close to the Giza pyramids came across the final resting place of an ancient Egyptian official called Pet-et-ty. Entombed with him was the body of his wife, Nesey-seker. The archaeologists were bemused by the tomb, since it contained two different curses. Drawings (hieroglyphs) found on the wall of the tomb revealed Pet-et-ty's curse, in which he calls on crocodiles, lions, and hippopotamuses to devour anyone who dares to violate the tomb. Meanwhile Nesey-seker's curse enlists the aid of similar animals, adding scorpions and snakes to the list of perils facing any such violator. For 4,600 years the tomb had remained intact, until its discovery in October 1992. Man-sour Bauriak, the Egyptian antiquities inspector who was in overall charge of the excavations, later revealed that when Pet-et-ty and Nesey-seker's tomb was opened and disturbed, a number of things began to go wrong. One of the tomb inspectors had his home destroyed by an earthquake; an experienced photographer was injured when his ladder collapsed into Pet-et-ty's burial chamber; a train carrying material away from the site derailed.

Are such incidents evidence of a curse, or pure coincidence? It was Howard Carter, the archaeologist and great denouncer of curses, who once wrote that 'all sane people should dismiss such inventions with contempt.' Despite his protestations, we now know that prior to his death he lived in fear of the gods of the Egyptian afterlife, in particular Anubis. Carter was undoubtedly wracked by guilt about his own role in the opening of the tomb of King Tutankhamun.

Stories of the curse persisted, and they continue to do so, as the public clamour for every sinister detail associated with stories that might reveal the existences of curses. In 2007 it was reported that an unnamed German man had returned a plundered ancient Egyptian carving to its rightful home, as he believed it had fatally cursed his family. The relic had been stolen a few years earlier from its resting place the Valley of Kings. The man had wanted to steal it and take it home to Germany as a souvenir of his trip. It was during the return journey to Europe that his troubles began. According to an anonymous note that accompanied the carving when it was returned to the Egyptian embassy in Berlin in 2004, the thief was struck down by inexplicable fatigue and a fever that progressed to paralysis, and ultimately caused his death. His family was aware that this once fit and healthy man had become ill only after stealing the piece, and so the stolen item was returned the Egyptians by his stepson, who believed that the thief's torment would not end with death, and that the artifact would continue to cause harm to the immediate family until it was returned. By returning the carving to Egypt's Supreme Council for Antiquities he hoped his stepfather's soul could rest in peace and his remaining family could live happy and contented lives.

In 2011, I was told of another family who had suffered from what they believed to be the curse of the pharaohs. They have requested anonymity so cannot be named, but they live in Florida, USA. In 1998 the head of the family, who was a retired serviceman, travelled to

Egypt to assist a close friend on an archaeological dig. He was not an archaeologist, but he had a mild interest in ancient Egyptian history and welcomed the opportunity to not only visit the country, but also to broaden his knowledge and experience. The dig site was at Luxor (Thebes) and the man was given menial tasks to help make the work of the genuine team of archaeologists simpler. One day he explored the site on his own and wandered a short distance outside the temple. Warm, he sat down for a rest by one of the sphinx statues that lined an ancient avenue leading to the temple. There he was approached by a local man who asked if he had a cigarette. He handed over a cigarette and his lighter, and the man sat down beside him. He was asked if he was interested in purchasing genuine artifacts from the tombs; smaller, easily transported items. He said that he was and told the man he would not be prepared to pay much for the items he wanted. The two men agreed to meet at the same time the next day and that they would come alone.

The American thought that this was probably a trick often played on unsuspecting tourists, and was sure that the items would be fake. He told his friend of the encounter, and he was warned about the perils of buying plastic artifacts and carrying large amounts of money. The following day, he met the local man again to look at the items. The American described them as: 'a couple of yellow (gold) coloured bird statues, some old papyrus with hardly legible hieroglyphics written on them, and lots of jewellery, three amulets and various rings of yellow metal, some of which had stones inset in them'. They agreed a price for one of the amulets, which bore the image of a scarab beetle, and two rings, the American selecting these because he thought them less 'tacky' than the rest of the goods offered. He paid over 100 US dollars, which he thought good value for both parties. The Egyptian bade him farewell and warned him to keep the scarab amulet securely locked inside a case, and never to carry it on his person outside Egypt, as it possessed the soul of death itself. Laughing, the man put each of the items he had purchased in his pocket and returned to the dig site within the temple. There he showed his friend what he had bought. His friend gave the objects a cursory glance, commenting that they looked better than the usual touristy objects and that they had a look of authenticity about them.

Back at his hotel that evening, the American placed his purchases on a table and prepared himself for dinner. He gave no further thought to items until the early hours of the morning, when he was awakened from a deep sleep by the chattering sound of insects. Thinking it was outside his room window, he got up and checked that it was closed and returned to his bed. Moments later he heard the chattering sound once more; this time it sounded close to the pillow. He searched the bed and then the room, but could find nothing that could warrant such a noise. He got no further sleep. At breakfast, his friend commented on how tired he looked, and noticed a trickle of blood running from his friend's nose. In the days that followed the American became so weak he was hardly able to get out of bed. With just two days of the trip remaining, it was decided that he should stay in his room and rest. If the sickness persisted when he got home he could seek medical help there.

That night the exhausted man was awakened by something in his room. When he opened his eyes he saw a tall, angry-looking animal-headed figure standing by his bed. Slowly the creature bent over him; it felt ice cold when it touched his skin. The prostrate man screamed in terror and the figure disappeared. The following morning the American caught sight of himself in a mirror and was shocked. His eyes had sunk back into their sockets and his face was skeletal; his skin was turning yellow. A doctor was called and told him he had a fever. He was prescribed medication and given dietary advice. The doctor warned that if he did not improve then he might be unable to fly back to America. That night his friend stayed by his side and saw an noticeable improvement, so he was able to return home.

Back in America, the man's health gradually stabilised, but his nightmares got worse. In his dreams he saw the god Anubis crouched over him, as another man, whom he described as a high priest, removed his innards and placed them in jars. The man often became hysterical, claiming to see evil spirits and loathsome creatures everywhere: in his home, in supermarkets and even at a cemetery. Doctors could do nothing and it was a local priest who suggested an exorcism to cleanse the soul. This was done, and those that conducted the ceremony admitted to hearing foreign voices, speaking in a vile tongue, emanating from the body of the man. A great shadow suddenly appeared on the walls of the room: an animal-headed man holding something in its hand. The infected man suddenly sat up and yelled out 'the great god of the dead walks among us, he commands you to leave him be or to suffer pain for all eternity.' He then fell back on to the bed in a coma-like state. The atmosphere within the room then lightened and it was believed that the spirit had been exorcised.

The man slowly recovered and, believing that his illness had started after he bought the amulet and rings, he decided to get rid of them and gave them to a friend. Within days, the friend became very ill and had to be placed in an asylum due to the hallucinations he suffered. He claimed to see the ancient dead walking in file behind the god Anubis. The man's wife took ill and almost died after being bitten by an insect and getting an infection, and the family car was stolen and crashed. Windows in their home began to crack and the smell of death seemed to linger in the upstairs rooms. Eventually, the original purchaser of the amulet and rings decided to get rid of the Egyptian items once and for all. He wrapped them in linen, saturated this with holy water and buried them deep in a specially prepared hole in an area of woodland. Once this was done, the health of the man in the asylum improved and he was able to return home. Two years later, he told a relative (who related the story to me). The relative persuaded him to take him to where the items had been buried because he felt they should be returned to Egypt through the local museum. When they visited the burial site, there was nothing to be found but a hole. The linen and the items were gone.

To this day the family monitors the local news stations, expecting to hear of further sinister activity created by the missing items of jewellery. The whereabouts of the items is unknown and despite efforts to locate them, through newspaper adverts and word of mouth, no trace of them has been found. The family is convinced that the items were well hidden that it would be virtually impossible for someone to have stumbled upon them. They believe that some kind of power or magic connected to the ancient Egyptian gods has recovered them.

There are many other recorded instances of strange happenings relating to Egyptian artifacts, including one that was reported in 2013. A ten-inch statue of Neb-Sanu, dating back almost 4,000 years, which is on display in a glass case at Manchester Museum, seemingly turned of its own accord. Time-lapse video footage appears to show the statue turning round. Immediately talk of an ancient curse began to circulate in the media. Tales of how dead spirits can use statues or effigies as alternative 'vessels' became popular, and the museum's own Egyptologist even suggested a curse was the cause of the phenomenon. Several more 'reasoned' explanations were offered, and the authorities quite rightly opted to accept that the movement was caused by vibration from a nearby road, or the movement of visitors within the museum. All of this proves that we are still fascinated by tales of curses, and in particular those that can come from the Egyptian pharaohs' tombs.

One man who thought he had solved the mystery of the curse was physician and biologist at Cairo University Dr Ezzeddin Taha, who examined archaeologists and employees of museums housing Egyptian artifacts. His findings showed that many staff had been exposed to a fungus that could cause fever-induced inflammation of the respiratory system. He observed how archaeologists suffered from what was known as the 'Coptic Itch'. This was linked to rashes of the skin and laboured breathing. The symptoms had been noted in people who had worked intensively with Egyptian papyri. Taha was able to prove the existence of a series of dangerous disease agents, among them *aspergillus niger*. His research, however, could not show whether the fungus was able to survive in mummies, or in grave chambers for periods of 1,000 years or more. Believing his findings to be a worthy news story, on 3 November 1962 Dr Taha held a press conference, at which he claimed to have discovered the cause of the curse of the pharaohs, or at least one cause. He said:

> *This discovery, has once and for all destroyed the superstition that explorers who worked in ancient tombs died as a result of some kind of curse. They were victims of morbific agents encountered at work. Some people may still believe that the curse of the pharaohs can be attributed to some supernatural powers, but that belongs to the realm of fairy tales.*

Taha admitted, however, that infections might not be the only cause of the deaths of so many scientists.

Soon after this press conference, Dr Taha and two of his co-workers were driving on the desert road between Suez and Cairo. It was quiet and empty. About 70 kilometres from Cairo, on a straight road, Taha's car suddenly swerved to the left, directly into the path of an oncoming vehicle. Taha and his companions died instantly from the impact. The occupants of the other vehicle were badly injured and able to give evidence about what had happened. According to the autopsy, Dr Taha had suffered 'a circulatory collapse'. And so the mysterious events continue.

As a result of Taha's work, many scholars, scientists and academics have tried to identify the reasons why so many deaths are associated with the opening of tombs or work on mummies and artifacts. It does seem that many archaeologists or people associated with that type of work have died prematurely. It seems likely that ancient Egyptian priests and magicians used advanced technical knowledge to retain a stranglehold of power over the people – instilling in them a fear of curses. Assessing just how advanced the Egyptians were as a scientific civilisation is difficult, since it appears that in ancient Egypt such knowledge was shrouded in secrecy, with only a select few practitioners understanding it and passing their craft on to following generations. They certainly had sophisticated medical knowledge, since there is evidence of bones and joints being set, broken bones being placed in splints and that the concept of sterilisation existed. Tubes, made from reeds wrapped in linen, were used for artificial nourishment, and forms of dental bridges fastened with gold wire were in use. To help the healing process, medicinal prescriptions were provided, mainly comprising juices, salves, powders and suppositories. Instructions for the taking of pills and other drugs produced by Egyptian doctors have survived and since been translated; incredibly, these bear a real similarity to those of modern pharmacology. The workers at the great pyramids were fed a diet of radishes, onions and leeks. The reasoning behind this was practical: with such large numbers of men working together there was a real hygiene problem. Any kind of epidemic would spread quickly and exterminate many in a short time. The vegetables would help prevent serious infections from breaking out. It has since been proved through modern research that the use of such a diet is effective against infectious agents such as *Streptococci*, *Staphylococci* and *Pneumococci*.

It is evident that the ancient Egyptians had a good understanding of the physiological effects of bacterial infection. As we know today, *Staphylococci* can produce pus that is able to infect the skin, kidneys and bone marrow, while *Streptococci* can cause diphtheria, blood poisoning and scarlet fever. So is it feasible that scientific secrets form part of the explanation for the curse of the pharaohs? The Egyptians knew of a type of nerve poison. Ergot is a grain fungus. One doctor believed that a poison was placed in the tombs by the high priests. After the final work on the tomb was completed and the workmen had left, the priests would sprinkle poison over everything that was in the tomb. Any intruder would inhale the poison and die. The use or knowledge of poison is as old as civilisation itself. Some 4,000 years ago, the very first pharaoh, Menes, grew poisonous plants and had their effects documented. It should also be noted that the Romans, who knew of Egyptian achievements in toxicology, acquired most of their poisons from Egypt. Caligula, Claudius, Nero and Caracalla were said to possess large collections of poisons. There are also natural poisons to be considered, such as those from snake and insect venom. These could be drawn from the creature and stored. The pharaohs' tombs, which ultraviolet rays could not penetrate, would be ideal environments for storing poisons and maintaining their effectiveness. An archaeologist need not have oral contact with any such poison. To be effective, some of the poisons need only brush or penetrate the skin. In pharaohs' tombs, powerful poisons such as aconite, arsenic, and conium may have been used to paint walls and artifacts. Their potency was, and is, long-lasting. It has been suggested that poisonous gases and vapours, in precipitated form, were most likely present in the tombs. In the airtight chambers these vapours could precipitate and remain there until released by the tomb being opened.

One closely guarded poison of ancient Egypt was quicksilver (mercury). As quicksilver easily evaporates at very low temperatures, it is a dangerous poison. The danger to a victim is further enhanced because its vapors are odourless, but damage the nervous system. Then we have prussic acid, a colourless liquid, which causes death from choking. The Egyptians isolated this deadly poison from peach pits.

Some scholars believe that mummy bandages were initially soaked in a mix of prussic acid and volatile oils. This would also account for the widespread decomposition of royal mummies.

Science has long been searching for a rational explanation for the curse, with many scientists pursuing the possibility of infection. One was South African geologist Dr John Wiles. In October 1956, Wiles clambered into the subterranean grottoes of the Rhodesian mountains. He had no idea that in doing so he might be exposing himself to mortal danger. His role was to examine the application of bat excrement, which is similar to guano, for use as a fertiliser. Wiles descended to about 450 feet and was startled by a sudden noise. The pitch-black roof of the grotto suddenly came to life, as thousands of bats that hung there moved and squeezed closer together. Wiles ascended as quickly as he could. Within a few days he was complaining of indigestion, aching muscles, and running a high fever. His doctor diagnosed him as suffering from pneumonia and pleurisy. He was prescribed drugs, but the treatment didn't work and his condition grew worse. Wiles was then admitted to Geoffrey Hospital in Port Elizabeth. One of the directors at the hospital, Dr Dean, recalled that a disease had recently been discovered that was prevalent among explorers who had been visiting Inca caves in Peru. Dean took a blood sample from Wiles, whose condition was fast failing, and forwarded it to the United States for examination and assessment. Within hours, confirmation was received that the geologist was suffering from histoplasmosis, a disease caused by an infectious fungus which grows in bat excrement and other rotting matter. Antibiotics were administered and Wiles recovered. Dr Dean then wondered if the same disease might be a cause of the puzzling deaths connected with the pharaohs' tombs. The rock-based tombs would be an ideal breeding ground for such bacteria.

Combustion is often observed on royal mummies, as a direct result of bacteriological processes. The fats, oils, and resins that are smothered on the mummy begin to decompose and they produce heat, which we now know leads to the mysterious charring of the corpse. For countless decades, archaeologists pondered why mummies were so blackened in appearance. The cause is bacteria. Chemists and bacteriologists believe that bacteria can survive, under the right conditions, for centuries; so it is not inconceivable that the ancient

Egyptians used bacterial cultures that would produce poisonous gases to protect the royal tomb.

In 1986, French doctor of medicine Caroline Stenger-Phillip believed she had found an explanation for the mysterious deaths that were attached to tombs and the mummy. Stenger-Phillip believed that food offerings left in tombs before they were sealed would create ideal mould-growing conditions. Since much of the food left consisted of fruit and vegetables, it was highly likely that these objects grew mould, which in turn and over time would form organic dust particles. The dust particles could have had a high allergenic potency. Dr Stenger-Phillip further believed that many of the archaeologists who had forced entry into sealed tombs for the first time suffered an allergic reaction after breathing and inhaling these dust particles, which ultimately led to their deaths. Recent studies have revealed that many ancient mummies do harbour mould, including at least two potentially dangerous species: *Aspergillus niger* and *Aspergillus flavus*. These moulds can cause allergic reactions ranging from nasal congestion to bleeding in the lungs. The toxins themselves can be extremely harmful to people with weakened immune systems. Another doctor, Italian physician Nicola di Paolo, carried out her own research and arrived at a similar conclusion. Di Paolo identified another possible fungus, *Aspergillus ochraceus*, at Egyptian archaeological sites. *Aspergillus ochraceus* has been shown to produce some mycotoxins, including *Penicillic acid*, *Ochratoxin A*, *Xanthomeginin*, *Viomellein* and *Vioxanthin*.

In 1999, a German microbiologist, Gottard Kramer, from the Univerity of Leipzig, revealed that he believed the cause of the pharaohs' curse was mould spores. Kramer had analyzed 40 mummies and identified a number of potentially dangerous spores. Mould spores are resilient and tough and can survive for thousands of years, especially in a dark, dry tomb. Although most spores are harmless, a few can be toxic. Kramer also noted that mould spores were found in dirt samples collected from tombs. He believes that when the tombs were initially opened and fresh air blew inside, these mould spores would be blown up into the air and circulate. When spores enter the human body, through the nose, mouth or mucous membranes, they can trigger severe and occasionally fatal illnesses of the lungs, organs and intestines, leading to organ failure or death, particularly in individuals with weakened immune systems (including many of the original visitors who are reported to have visited the tomb of King Tutankhamun on or shortly after its opening). Today, for this very reason, scientists and archaeologists wear protective masks and gloves when unwrapping or examining a mummy. Back in the 1920s no protection was worn.

To supplement the work of Dr Kramer, another German practitioner, Dr Hans Merk, who was a dermatologist at the University of Aachen, Germany, performed similar research and he fully agrees with Dr Kramer's conclusions. Merk relates how he analysed dust and rock samples from different tombs and found three main types of mould: *Aspergillus flavus, Aspergillus terreus* and *Cephalosporium (Acremonium)*. Each of these species is toxic, particularly to the elderly and those who are immune deficient.

Mould spores are not only found in ancient Egyptian tombs. In fact, the most notorious case of the 'mummy's curse' was in Poland, in 1973, with the opening of the tomb of King Casimir IV. A team of twelve research scientists were granted permission to break open the tomb of Casimir IV, king of Poland from 1447–92, so that they could examine his remains, with restoration being the ultimate objective. On Friday 13 April 1973, the tomb was opened. All twelve researchers were present. Inside, they found a wooden coffin that had badly deteriorated. It was heavily rotted but still in place within the tomb. Within just a few days of the opening, four of the twelve scientists had died. Shortly thereafter a further six died, and only two survivors remained. One of these was research microbiologist Dr B. Smyk. He had serious problems with his equilibrium in the five years that followed, but he was able to perform some detailed microbiological examinations of the tomb to see if there were any correlations between his illness, the deaths and anything sinister found within the tomb. Dr Smyk found various types of fungi on the artifacts that had been removed from the tomb by the research team. He identified three specific species: *Aspergillus flavus, Penicillium rubrum* and *Penicillium rugulosum*. These fungi can produce mycotoxins, and are believed to have caused the deaths of the other ten researchers. Since these findings were published, it has been further speculated that

111

similar fungi and spores may have been responsible for the death of Lord Carnarvon, who died a few months after exploring King Tutankhamun's tomb in 1923. When the mummy of Ramesses II (king of Egypt from 1304–1237 BC) was removed and transported to the Musee de l'Homme in Paris in 1976, over 370 fungal colonies belonging to eighty-nine different fungal species (including *Aspergillus*) were found growing in and on the mummy.

The main types of deadly spores prevalent in Egyptian burials are:

Aspergillus flavus: This fungus is associated with aspergillosis of the lungs and/or disseminated aspergillosis. It is occasionally identified as the cause of corneal, otomycotic and nasoorbital infections.

Aspergillus ochraceus: This fungus produces a kidney toxin, Ochratoxin A, which may produce ocratoxicosis in humans. The ochratoxin may also be produced by other *Aspergillus* and *Penicillium* species. Other toxins which can be produced by this fungus include penicillic acid, xanthomegnin and viomellein. These are all reported to be kidney and liver toxins.

Penicillium species: These fungi may cause hypersensitivity pneumonitis and allergic alveolitis in susceptible individuals. Some species can produce mycotoxins. It is a common cause of extrinsic asthmas (immediate-type hypersensitivity: type I) Acute symptoms include oedema and brochiospasms. Chronic cases may develop pulmonary emphysema.

Aspergillus terreus: This fungus produces the toxins patulin and citrinin that maybe associated with disease in humans and animals. It is associated with aspergillosis of the lungs and/or disseminated aspergillosis. It is found as an isolate from otomycosis (ear infection) and enychomycosis (infection of the finger or toenails).

Aspergillus niger: This fungus is the third most common species associated with invasive pulmonary aspergillosis. It is also often a causative agent of aspergilloma and is the most frequently encountered agent of otomycosis.

Cephalosporium (Acremonium) species: Some of this species are recognized as opportunistic pathogens of humans and animals, causing mycetoma, onychomycosis, and hyalohyphomycosis. Clinical manifestations of hyalohyphomycosis caused by *Acremonium* include arthritis, osteomyelitis, peritonitis, endocarditis, pneumonia, cerebritis and subcutaneous infection.

As mould spores are protected by a tough, waterproof layer made of chitin, mould can survive for thousands of years. Prolonged exposure to toxic moulds, especially in an enclosed area such as a burial chamber or tomb, can potentially cause serious health problems. They can irritate, infect and ultimately damage the eyes, skin, lungs, mucous membranes, respiratory tract, stomach and intestines.

One inspector general of the Egyptian Antiquities administration was a man named Reginald Engelbach. While working near the Meidum pyramid, south of Cairo and on the edge of the western desert, Engelbach discovered an ancient tomb. Within the tomb's antechamber he found a curse tablet bearing the inscription: 'The spirit of the dead will wring the neck of a grave robber as if it were that of a goose.' The curse tablet referred to the spirit of the dead person officially buried there, and no one else. However, on further inspection Engelbach found two corpses within the chamber. The first and original corpse was mummified; this was the corpse for whom the tomb had been built. The second corpse was that of an intruder. From the position of the body and examination of the area where it lay, Engelbach suspected that the man had been killed by a stone that been designed to plummet from the ceiling as he stretched out his hand in an attempt to steal jewellery from the mummy, yet no trap was obvious. It was a mystery that later caused Engelbach to wonder whether the tomb robber had died as a result of the falling stone striking him on the head, or whether he had become a victim of the curse. We shall never know.

Chapter 11

The Sad End of
Walter Ingram

This swashbuckling and extraordinary tale of bravery and selflessness deserves to be told since it involves the mysterious curse-related death of one of England's greatest heroes. Part of the incredible story of Walter Herbert Ingram was first reported in an issue of *Strand* magazine in 1896.

Walter Herbert Ingram was born in 1855, the youngest son of Herbert Ingram, Member of Parliament for Boston, Lincolnshire, and founder and proprietor of the *Illustrated London News*. Walter was educated at Eton and Trinity College, Cambridge. At the age of 24 he visited South Africa, where he was involved in some of the violent events that led to the defeat of the Zulus, culminating in the Battle of Ulundi. Ingram, it is recorded, worked alongside John Dunn, the Chief of Intelligence on Lord Chelmsford's staff. Dunn was regarded as an extraordinary character who, having lived among the Zulus for more than thirty years, had personal and intimate knowledge of their race. During these three decades Dunn set himself up as a Petty Chieftain in King Cetswayo's confidence; he is also said to have sired over 160 children. At the end of the Zulu war, Ingram returned to England and purchased a lieutenancy in the 1st County of London Yeomanry, Middlesex Hussars.

Ingram assisted Lord Charles Beresford in the 1884–85 Soudan War. A short time later, in 1885, keen to support his compatriots, he returned to Africa having heard of the attempts to raise the siege of Khartoum. The ultimate goal was to rescue General Gordon. By the time Ingram got to Egypt the expedition was weeks ahead of him, but he was determined to follow and catch up. He purchased a steam launch and employed an engineer and an Arab boy as his crew. This tiny group passed through the Suez and Sweetwater canals to reach Cairo, then continued along the Nile. The Arab boy was of no assistance, and deserted early on in the journey. While ascending the cataract at Dal serious problems occurred, which might have deterred any normal person from continuing the journey. Walter Ingram, however, simply took the problems in his stride. At Dal the steam launch capsized in turbulent waters, throwing Ingram and the engineer into the rapids. The engineer, being unable to swim, had to be rescued by Ingram, who swam to his aide and pulled him ashore. Ingram then dived back into the water and incredibly was able to salvage the upturned vessel. The engine was full of water, so Ingram opted to discard it and instead he rigged a sail. The engineer was exhausted, so Ingram continued the journey to Korti alone, a distance of nearly 500 miles. He negotiated two further cataracts single-handed.

At Korti Ingram caught up with the expedition he was chasing, and quickly struck up a friendship with Lord Charles Beresford, who commanded the sixty-one strong Naval Brigade. The British force, 1,200 men in total, was suffering in the sweltering hot climate and in desperate need of fresh water as they marched towards conflict at Howeiyat, Jakdul Wells and Abu Klea. The first two of these offered no resistance and were occupied without opposition, allowing the men time to recover. However, the respite was to be short-lived, and at dawn on 17 January 1885 the British encampment came under fire from Dervishes situated on the nearby hills. The British troops were mustered to form a marching square, with the wounded and sick personnel protected in the centre of the square. Meanwhile the Naval Brigade, of which Ingram was now a member, was tasked with operating and supporting the Gardner quick-firing gun that was positioned within the rear element of the square. At around 10am, the square began to advance towards Abu Klea: three miles to be covered under the most difficult of circumstances as the square was attacked and shot at. Barely half an hour into this advance, an army of approximately 10,000 Arabs, some on foot and many on horseback, began to converge on the square. Orders were given to British troops to try to reach a small area of high ground nearby, but the square was no longer secure on all four sides. It was beginning to disintegrate, making it vulnerable. Lord Beresford had the Gardner gun run outside of the square and instructed it to open fire on the attacking maniacal Dervishes; the result was carnage as the bullets cut swathes through the charging Arabs. The Dervishes were clearly disheartened by the loss of so many men, but then the gun jammed and the assault on the British was reinvigorated. Frantic attempts were made to fix the weapon, but during these two of the gun party were speared and Beresford was knocked off his feet. Eight other sailors protecting the gun were killed by the oncoming hordes, and at least as many others were badly wounded.

Eventually the men reached the area of elevated ground and the gun was repaired, allowing volley fire that temporarily forced the Arabs back. The attacks, however, were relentless and eventually the Dervishes were able to break through the gaps. Dozens of camels were killed during the fighting; when alive they had formed part of a protective wall surrounding the rear of the marching human square. Face-to-face armed combat ensued. Ordered discipline was restored among the British troops and soon a further volley of fire forced back the Arabs, who hastily retreated. Walter Ingram was part of the front rank of troops, and Lord Beresford recorded in his own papers that (Ingram) was a 'keen soldier... at one time he was outside the square at Abu Klea, but always cool and collected, using his rifle with good effect. Many of us noticed his gallantry and his quiet determined manner.'

After Abu Klea, Lord Beresford obtained a temporary commission for Ingram, as a lieutenant in the Navy. Beresford had suffered huge losses to his fighting force during the battle, with many of his officers either been killed or wounded. Beresford had been wounded too, and while he underwent surgery Walter Ingram took on the role of officer commanding. Having secured the water wells, it was then decided that two steamers were to be sent on to Khartoum, but they arrived too late to rescue General Gordon. When the troops made the return voyage, one of the two steamers on which they travelled (the *Talahawiyeh*) struck a rock and had to be abandoned. Two days later the second steamer (the *Bordein*) also struck a rock, and was so badly damaged that it was forced to run ashore on a small island.

When information about the stranding of both vessels reached the main force, which had been stationed at Gubat, a rescue party consisting of nine officers (including Ingram) and twenty specially selected marksmen set off, in the steamer *Safieh*. The *Safieh* was well armed, having two Gardner guns and a four-pounder brass mountain gun on board. The rescue party set off on 1 February and made good progress; within two days they were in sight of the *Bordein*. There was just one major problem: to reach the *Bordein* they had to pass within yards of a heavily-armed fort at Wad Habeshi. Further fighting and loss of life was inevitable. The *Safieh* opened fire on the fort, and for a brief time it appeared she would escape without damage, but then she was hit by a stray shell that pierced a boiler, causing her to have to pull in for urgent repairs. The crew worked into the night, under gun fire from the nearby garrison. The steamer returned a steady stream of retaliatory fire, and Walter Ingram manned the Gardner gun. Eventually, the repairs were completed and the stranded men from the stricken *Bordein* were picked up from a prearranged rendezvous point and successfully returned to Gubat. Lord Beresford commended Ingram for his part in the rescue operation, during which many lives had been lost.

As a souvenir of his time in Egypt and his adventures there, Walter Ingram purchased a mummy for the princely sum of £50 from the English Consul at Luxor and had it shipped back to England, where it was unrolled and examined at the British Museum. Within the wrappings, papyri were found, including a blood-curdling curse, which appealed to the powers above to deny burial to the remains of the sacrilegious ghoul who disturbed the eternal sleep of the pharoah's corpse. The curse said that 'not one bone should remain with another, but that they should be swept to the sea', so as to render the reconstitution of the offender's body impossible.

Soon after sending the mummy back to England, Walter Ingram and Sir Henry Meux were on an elephant shoot in Somaliland. The natives brought them a large chunk of dried earth, claiming it to be the spoor of the biggest elephant in the world. The men interviewed the natives and were soon on the march, hunting down a herd of elephants just outside Berbera in Somaliland. Eventually, on 6 April 1888, they caught sight of the herd, only for Sir Henry to realise his elephant gun was still back at camp. Unselfishly, Ingram offered his own gun to his friend, leaving himself with only a small-bore rifle. The men used tried and tested tactics to kill their prey. Sir Henry took the lead and followed the bull of the herd, while Ingram focused on felling one of the lesser cows. It was a perilous situation but Ingram displayed ingenuity. He realised that by galloping his horse close to the elephant, he was able to get close enough to fire a shot and then wheel away. He believed that he could tire the creature, eventually forcing her to fall due to a large number of small shots rather than one cleverly-aimed shot from an elephant gun.

Focusing on the elephant instead of his course, Ingram was knocked from his saddle when his horse ran beneath the drooping bough of a tree. He was dazed and without any form of defence, having dropped his rifle. The wounded elephant saw his vulnerability and stopped in her tracks; slowly, she turned to face him. The roles of hunter and hunted were reversed. The elephant approached Ingram, who lay on the ground. The Somali servant assisting him claimed he heard a haunting chanting that seemed to fill the air around them. He said that Ingram looked terrified, as though he could see something beyond the elephant cow. The servant desperately tried to save Ingram, moving closer to the injured man and firing close-range shots into the angry elephant, which he said appeared to possessed by some malevolent spirit. Never before had he witnessed an elephant exhibit such manic and vicious behaviour. He fired several rounds into its ear with no response. Nothing, it seemed, would prevent the creature from exacting its revenge for the pain it had suffered. As the servant watched, the great elephant trampled Ingram into the ground. Once Ingram had died, the haunting sound of chanting disappeared.

For several days the elephant remained at the spot, refusing to allow anyone to approach. Eventually, she left Ingram's crushed and rapidly decomposing remains where he had fallen, and they were gathered up and buried in what was thought to be a stony valley, but was later discovered to be a dried-up ravine. Several months later, an organised expedition was arranged by the dead man's brother, Sir William Ingram, which travelled along the coast in an attempt to recover the body. For days the expedition searched the area where the body had been interred. They found only one sock, part of a human bone and a few buttons torn from his garments that had been scattered among stones nearby, but no skeleton and no further clothing. These few relics were subsequently interred at Aden with full military honours.

It wasn't long before observers made the connection between the curse that had been found in the wrappings of Ingram's mummy, and the circumstances of his death and burial. When the curse was discovered, Ingram had laughed and mocked the idea. Yet now his bones had been swept away by the force of a river and potentially carried out to sea, 'never be reconstituted into their original skeletal form'. Had the curse struck again?

It was said that Ingram's mummy later came into the possession of Lady Valerie Meux, who was an avid collector of Egyptian artifacts and a friend of eminent Egyptologist Ernest Wallis Budge. Her collection numbered over 1,700 pieces. She later claimed that her husband, Sir Henry Meux, had later come by the tusks of the elephant that killed Ingram. She was, it appears, a believer in the 'unexplained' or supernatural, and this also interested her friend, Ernest Wallis Budge. It is claimed she said that her husband believed the elephant tusks to be possessed by the spirit of some ancient Egyptian god, and that in certain moments they both saw 'an Egyptian spirit' standing before them. Because of his aristocratic background, Sir Henry would never discuss such matters with anyone other than his wife; though it is said that he feared being cursed. Apparently the writer Rudyard Kipling heard this tale while visiting a London club, and retold every grisly detail to fellow writer Rider Haggard, who in turn recounted it on many occasions, no doubt embellishing every detail for each audience he held. In another version, Walter Ingram returned home having located the mummy of Queen Nesmin. Opening the casket in the offices of the *Illustrated London News*, he discovered an inscription, 'May the person who unwraps me die rapidly'. By quirk of fate, Walter Ingram's nephew, Bruce Ingram, later take became editor of the *Illustrated London News*. During his tenure he reported every detail of Howard Carter's discovery and excavation of King Tutankhamen's tomb. Carter gave a small statue of Anubis to Bruce Ingram as a gift. He had in fact stolen it from the tomb during the find. In turn, Bruce bequeathed it to his nephew Michael, who passed it on to his grandson Matt.

Chapter 12

The Curious Tale of
Isaiah Deck

Isaiah Deck was the son of a highly respected geologist, also called Isaiah Deck. Isaiah junior was born in England, but for many years lived in New York. Following in his father's footsteps, he was a geologist by profession and also held a keen interest in archaeology. In 1847, Isaiah Deck junior made one of many visits to Egypt. He was originally in search of Cleopatra's lost emerald mines, but was soon distracted by something altogether different, conceiving an incredible plan that nowadays would be viewed as an act of sacrilege. It was more through need than desire that he enacted his plan; he aimed to address America's desperate shortage of rags for paper-making. Deck saw an abundance of mummies during his visits to tombs and burial grounds in Egypt, but rather than consider and respect them as human remains, he looked at the mummy wrappings as a potential source of rags for paper. He wrote:

So numerous are they in some localities out of the usual beaten tracks of most travellers, that after the periodical storms whole areas may be seen stripped of sand, and leaving fragments and limbs exposed in such plenty and variety.

Assume two thousand years of widespread embalming, an average lifespan of thirty-three years and a stable population of eight million. This would leave you with about five hundred million mummies. Add to that the number of mummified animals including cats, bulls and crocodiles, and the number drastically rises. It is by no means rare to find above 30lbs weight of linen

121

wrappings on mummies… One from the collection of Mr Davidson yielded, when unravelled, nearly 300 yards, and weighed, when bleached, nearly 32lbs. A princess from the late Mr Pettigrew's collection [an American showman totally unconnected to Dr Pettigrew of London] *was swathed in 40 thicknesses, producing 42 yards of the finest texture. The supply of linen rags would not be limited to the mummies of the human species alone; independent of that obtainable from this source, a more than equal amount of cloth could be depended on from the mummies of the sacred bulls, crocodiles, ibises, and cats, as all of these animals were embalmed and swathed in a superior quality of linen… some bandages, from five inches to five feet wide, and five yards long have been stripped from mummies their entire length without tearing.*

Deck further calculated the average consumption of paper in America to be about 15lbs per person per year. This meant that the supply from Egyptian mummies would be able to keep up with the American demand for about fourteen years, by which point a substitute supply source or material would likely have been discovered, rendering the need for rags unnecessary. Thus he immediately set about shipping tons of Egyptian mummies across the Atlantic to America, for the sole purpose of making paper pulp from the linen wrappings (he published a paper on it in 1855). It seems that this was done on an experimental scale, and one newspaper (the Syracuse *Sentinel*) is said to have printed at least two of its editions on recycled mummy linen. Unfortunately, unlike the mummies, no copies of the papers have survived.

During this same period, America had become more aware of Egyptian mummies as a type of novelty. Many mummies were put on show in museums and travelling shows across the country, such as those displayed by Mr Pettigrew, who amused his audience by unwrapping the mummy and manipulating the skeletal remains. Elsewhere collecting Egyptian mummies was becoming a hobby for the rich. Dr Thomas Joseph Pettigrew, a noted London physician (he was also surgeon to the Duke of Kent and the Duke of Sussex) was one such collector; he held private parties where he would entertain his guests by unwrapping a mummy or displaying other curiosities. Pettigrew went on to write the *History of Egyptian Mummies* (1834), which is still referred to today. It is recorded that people flocked to watch Dr Pettigrew unwrap a mummy at the Royal College of Surgeons in London. So popular was the event that even the Archbishop of Canterbury was turned away.

For many years, Deck junior had evaluated other sources of material for paper-making, including aloe, plantain, banana and dagger-grass, but none of these proved suitable. He was aware of Egyptian artifacts and his interest in archaeology had come from his father, who had been on friendly terms with Giovanni Belzoni, described by some as an 'infamous Italian robber of Egyptian tombs'. Belzoni gave Deck senior many authentic Egyptian artifacts and objects from his private collection, including a statue of the god Osiris, and a piece of linen claimed to be authentic mummy wrapping. It was claimed that friends of Isaiah Deck senior said he would often speak of the feeling that something malevolent was attached to some of the objects Belzoni had given him, in particular the statue of Osiris, which had been given with the stern warning, 'Think no ill will of any man before it!' While Deck senior dismissed such ideas as foolish, he nevertheless felt that the statue had an unexplainable presence that set the mood of the house. Deck senior believed that since Belzoni had stolen the artifacts from tombs or purchased them from dubious sources, including known grave plunderers and robbers, the wrath of the gods had been incurred. His staff often spoke of hearing strange voices whispering in a foreign tongue and in an agitated manner.

One male member of the household staff fell seriously ill and became blind after he called the statue, which was a constant talking point within the household, 'a piece of useless rubbish that held no more mystical power than his big toe'. Then, foolishly some might say, he picked up the statue and commanded it to speak or move. When it didn't, he replaced it on the shelf exclaiming, 'It has no eyes, so it cannot see, it has no ears, so it cannot hear, it has no heart, so it cannot feel any emotion. It cannot do anything but look its ugly self.' The man had previously been in good health, but that night he suffered dreadful nightmares, screaming for help and demanding that the black dog of death be removed from sitting on his chest. As he grew more delirious, he was screamed that the black dog was clawing at his face and gouging at his eyes. Yet no blood appeared on his face or around his eyes. It is said that when he awoke, he could see nothing, and was insane. The doctors who examined him could find no reason for the illness or the sudden blindness. Naturally, such matters were never divulged to the public or press. Isaiah Deck junior, however, was quick to try resolve matters, and immediately took possession of the statue and other curiosities, thereby returning some normality to his father's home. Deck senior said that with the artifacts gone, (presumably to America with his son) the entire atmosphere in the house changed for the better. The whereabouts of the statue now are unknown.

Chapter 13

More Mummy Wrappings

It would seem that Isaiah Deck was not alone in his belief that mummy wrappings could be effectively recycled into paper. In another bizarre case, American industrialist Isaac Augustus Stanwood bought tons of mummy linen so that he could pulp it and make it into paper at his Maine-based plant. Stanwood claimed that because there were so many mummies available across Egypt, with each one being wrapped in 20lbs of cloth or more, and Egypt was a poor country, he had hit on a perfect way to make a lot of money.

The *Portland Sunday Telegram* published details and sketches of the mummies arriving by ship at Portland harbour, from where they were transported in large cases by horse cart to the plant. Once there, the mummies were tossed on to elongated benches where they were unceremoniously opened. No real care was taken by the handlers when they removed the woven linen bindings, which were thrown into a barrow and transferred to vats where they were reduced to pulp, thereafter being made into heavy brown wrapping paper. It appears that the gums and oils used by the ancient Egyptians during the embalming process added value to the papermaking process. Once the wrappings had been removed, the skeletal remains were discarded. Dozens of ancient skeletons were scattered across the floor. At the end of the working day the skeletons were put into a furnace.

Initially the plan seemed to work, but when it came to the paper production phase, the first of many problems arose. The initial issue facing Stanwood was that the mummy linen was so badly discoloured (various shades of brown and burnt orange) that it couldn't be used in the creation of white paper. Refusing to admit defeat, Stanwood instead resolved to make brown wrapping paper. This paper would then be sold to shops for wrapping products.

It is said that Stanwood met no resistance procuring and purchasing the mummies in Egypt. Indeed, on several occasions he had to bid against an Egyptian railroad manager to buy them! The Egyptian Government (Railways), he claimed, had used dried-out mummies as fuel in their locomotives for many years.

Stanwood's papermaking business came to an abrupt halt when a cholera epidemic ravaged the region, and Stanwood's 'mummy paper' was blamed. Workers at the plant who had been handling the mummies spoke of the disgusting odour of death that permeated the air for many miles around the plant. Others mentioned handling dark broken bones, some of which still had rotting flesh attached. One curious report was of an aggressive black dog that was frequently seen loitering in the plant area. The creature would stand and stare at the workers as they unwrapped the mummies. When one man tossed the animal a bone, it reared up its head and launched itself at him, savagely attacking and biting him, before being forced away by workers who came to the man's aid. The man who suffered the attack later died, his face contorted into a look of terror, and his eyes bulging from their sockets as if he were silently screaming. The workers were worried that the dog was still prowling the plant area, and many feared for their lives. Talk among the workers was that the dog was part of a curse, the harbinger of death.

The men knew that what they were doing was morally wrong: disturbing the dead and desecrating their tombs in order to make a profit. However, the management at the plant quelled all such talk, describing it as unfounded and ridiculous speculation. To put a permanent end to the damaging rumours, the managers ordered the dog to be shot – after all, it was a feral dog and had killed a worker. The dog was shot several times over a period of a few days, but nothing seemed to harm or kill it and it never showed signs of any suffering or injury. Poison traps were laid out, as were bear traps, but the creature remained alive. Eventually it was decided that the best way to destroy it was to starve it to death, so every possible source of nutrition was removed. Instead of wasting away, the animal remained fit and healthy. At times it was seen within a building in the plant that housed the skeletal remains; when approached it would snarl. When cholera broke out, the animal was seen one last time on a grass mound, howling to the heavens. Then it disappeared and was never seen again.

The plant was temporarily closed down by the authorities as the source of the cholera epidemic, and many men who worked there died. The local people maintained it was the curse of the pharaoh's tomb that had caused the deaths. It was later revealed that many of the wrapped mummies contained papyri, upon which Egyptian writing could be seen. These were assumed to be curses. We shall never know, because the papyri, along with everything else, were recklessly destroyed in the furnace.

America was not alone in its abuse of mummies. According to some nineteenth-century sources, tens of thousands of mummies were shipped to England, where they were used as fertiliser. Elsewhere it had become fashionable for socialites to hold dinner parties where guests would be entertained by the unwrapping of an authentic Egyptian mummy that had been privately purchased by the host. The tale would be told to the guests that the specific mummy was some ancient Egyptian god, an evil tormentor of souls. In life he had arranged for the execution of thousands of Egyptians, but in death he was entertainment for guests, who would pass round pieces of the skeleton. The remains were eventually disposed of by incineration, being burnt in the homes of the wealthy, while some of the bones were given to dogs of the street.

It is also known that in the latter part of the nineteenth century, Arabs would sell the powdered remains of mummies mixed with butter, as an ointment to heal all kinds of ailments, including bruises. Mummy trafficking was becoming a financially rewarding business, and became more widespread during this period. However, there had long been a trade in mummies. In 1580 one merchant, Mr John Sanderson, went to great lengths to purchase close to 600 pounds (270kg) of mummy flesh, for sale on the English market. The flesh was sold to the upper classes, who believed it had unique mystical medicinal powers that would heal all illnesses. In 1549, a priest to Queen Catherine de Medici of France had conducted a private expedition to Egypt. While there, the priest worked closely with a group of Italian doctors, breaking in to dozens of tombs around Saqqara, searching for mummified remains. Catherine's father-in-law,

King Frances I of France, forever fearing assassination, carried about his person a pouch containing ground-up mummy, mixed with ground rhubarb. The king believed this potion would heal him should he ever be wounded while out shooting.

Another king to use mummies to his own advantage was King Charles II, who had a store of mummies and would collect the dust that fell from the wrappings. He would then rub this on to his skin, believing the 'greatness' (of the dead pharaoh) would rub off and help him. Was he cursed for such outrageous behaviour? During his time on the English throne Charles witnessed many catastrophic events that caused great loss of life: the Great Plague of London, which saw an estimated 7,000 people die, followed by the Great Fire of London, which destroyed around 13,200 houses and 87 churches in the English capital. On 2 February 1685, King Charles II had an apoplectic fit and died suddenly. It was initially believed that he had been poisoned, a theory put forward by one of the royal doctors, although today it is claimed that the symptoms he displayed indicate that he potentially died of a kidney infection.

Mummy powder was in great demand in the seventeenth century, but there were many dangerous rogue mixtures being sold on the streets of Europe, in particular in France. So problematic was this issue that in 1694 French pharmacist Pierre Pomet offered advice to prospective purchasers of mummy powder: 'Look for one that is black without bones or dust, with a nice smell of something burnt rather than tar or resin'.

The original source of mummies came from Arab plunderers, who robbed graves in search of valuables such as jewellery or small statues. They were rogues, with no respect for the dead or living; the mummies were obstacles in the way of the treasure chests. Sometimes the tomb robbers would tear apart a mummy looking for hidden jewellery. As tomb robbery became more common, the tombs were designed to be more difficult to access once formally closed.

An excellent representation of the plight of a tomb robber comes from a story told by Ernest Wallis Budge. He recounted the tale of a party of Western treasure seekers who had a sticky surprise when they came across a tomb close to the pyramids near Cairo in around 1800. In the tomb they found a large sealed jar, which they opened and found to contain honey. Curiously, they were tempted to taste the honey, so one member of the party dipped a finger into the substance and tried it: it was indeed pure honey. They sent for some bread and a short time later began to eat the honey by dipping the bread into it. They thought that the centuries-old honey might have magical powers, and if not, at least it provided a splendid lunch. As they ate, one of the party noticed a hair floating on top of the honey. He tried to remove it, but was surprised to find it was attached to something else. He pulled the hair firmly and further hair appeared on the surface, which he grabbed and pulled from the jar. Out came the body of a fully dressed child, who had been placed in the jar and preserved in the honey! Needless to say, the party withdrew from the tomb in haste.

Chapter 14

The Mystery of Nesyamun

The mortal remains of one of Egypt's most important mummies, Nesyamun (originally called Natsef-Amun) are now in Leeds, West Yorkshire. The name Nesyamun means 'The one belonging to the God Amun'.

In life, and in death, Nesyamun has been involved in some horrific incidents, yet his body survives. His death remains something of mystery. He died during the reign of Ramesses XI (1113–1085 BC). When he died he was in his mid-forties. He was bald, and had well cared for and manicured hands and fingernails decorated with henna. He seems to have been a man who held a privileged position and lived a good life. When alive he measured just 5ft 6in tall and was employed as a 'Waab priest', which meant he had reached a certain level of purification and was therefore permitted to approach the statue of Amun in the most sacred inner sanctum of the temple. Part of his daily ritual would be to bath four times and shave twice. On his death, as was the custom, his body went through the mummification process and was buried in a tomb in the Deir el Bahri region of Egypt. There it lay undisturbed for 3,000 years until 1822, when it was unearthed during one of many tomb robberies carried out by a so-called 'antiquarian' named M.J. Passalacqua, who is said to have promoted himself as a specialist finding Egyptian artifacts for private buyers around the world.

A few months later, in 1823, Nesyamun was purchased by a Leeds banker called John Blades, who procured three mummies for the Leeds Philosophical and Literary Society, which had been founded in 1819 with the backing of influential professionals from the area: industrialist John Marshall, whose Holbeck mill had the façade of an Egyptian temple, surgeon Charles Thackrah and newspaper owner Edward Baines, to name but a few.

In 1828, amid something of a local sensation, the mummy of Nesyamun was unwrapped before an audience of notaries, the process being overseen by surgeon Thomas Pridgin Teale. A previous mummy owned by the society had disappointingly been found to have been eaten by beetles when it was unwrapped, so there was hope that the mummy of Nesyamun would be better preserved. The body was contained within two coffins. The outer coffin was constructed of sycamore, and was in the shape of a man with his arms crossed on his chest (coffins were pre-made in male and female forms). The face painted on the lid did not belong to Nesyamun: it was a generic image. Only the rich and powerful members of royal families could afford to have bespoke coffins decorated with their own likeness. The coffin, which had a yellow background, had been decorated with scenes and hieroglyphics from the *Book of the Dead*, intended to offer magical protection and enable Nesyamun to safely reach the underworld. There were about thirty such scenes on the coffin.

After carefully removing the body from the two coffins, the linen wrappings which covered the entire mummy were removed layer by layer, some forty layers in all. The outer wrappings were of finely woven, narrow linen of very good quality. As each layer was removed, the cloth became increasingly coarser and wider. Papyri, jewellery and tiny ornaments were found between some layers, which had been deliberately placed there for use by Nesyamun in the afterlife. One leather ornament could be dated to pinpoint the period during which he had died, and he was the only known surviving mummy from that period, making his existence of real importance for historical and scientific research.

When the final layer of wrapping was removed the group was surprised to find the body remained hidden from view. A deep layer of spices, including cinnamon, had been placed between the skin and the linen, measuring about one inch in depth. When removed, it was found that the spices had also been used to fill Nesyamun's abdominal and chest cavities. Shockingly, when his face was finally revealed it was incredibly intact. The hair on his head, his eyebrows and beard had been shaved off. Yet that wasn't what stunned the informal autopsy team; it was the facial disfigurement that caused alarm. The face was not that of a man who had died a peaceful death, but that of a man who had suffered a terrible and agonising death. His mouth was wide open and his tongue protruded from it. Only one other mummy has been found with a similar grimace. On closer examination, the throat had been stuffed with a powder created from vegetables, and the cheeks were filled out with sawdust so that the facial structure maintained a natural shape. The mummy was in truly excellent condition, and one member of the team, William Osburn, noted 'his skin was grey, in good condition, and soft and greasy to touch.'

The examination revealed much about Nesyamun in life, but nothing that could tell of his death, which had clearly been torturous. Some believed, because of the contorted face, that Nesyamun had been murdered. He could have been strangled to death, which would explain the elongated tongue emerging from the mouth (this also occurs during hanging). However, there was no obvious evidence of spinal fracture at the base of the neck, which discounts this theory. There the matter ended, and the mummy went on display at the museum, which was then located in Park Row.

The first tale connected to Nesyamun that I discovered came from the Grainger family, who once lived in Leeds. In the 1920s it seems that Roland Grainger was employed as a watchman in the district, and the museum in Park Row was one of the buildings he regularly monitored along with his colleagues. He would regale friends and family with 'off the record' stories of the mystical displays in the museum. One in particular relates to Nesyamun, and appears to be much more than just a 'ghost story'.

Grainger had been told by other watchmen that strange voices could be heard coming from the coffin: scratching sounds and sobbing. Dismissive of such talk, Grainger remained sceptical and put it down to the over-active imagination of his fellows. One evening, Roland approached the Nesyamun display and, intrigued by its history, stopped to look more closely at it. As he stood next to it he heard a strange scratching sound that appeared to emanate from within the coffin. Believing it to be mice or rodents, he resolved to report it to the curator. He was just about to move away when he heard whispering. He stopped in his tracks and turned to face the coffin. He was convinced that the whispering voice he could hear was a foreign man praying. Then came the sobbing! Roland stood for several moments, paralysed with fear and unable to move even his eyes. He swore that he saw some movement. Pulling himself together, he left the exhibit and the building. He told his family what had happened but they were incredulous, and asked him if he'd been drinking that evening. Grainger maintained that he was in complete control of his senses and that the incident had actually happened. However, since his own family didn't believe the story, he thought it pointless to report it to museum officials. For several weeks he went nowhere near the display, but still heard the sound of whispering prayers followed by sobbing.

Eventually a friend volunteered to come into the museum with Roland during his night time patrol, and to stand by the display and watch and listen while Roland went on his rounds. Once inside, both men heard the scratching sound and went to the display and stood in silence. The scratching stopped, to be replaced by a male voice that was whispering in a foreign tongue. Roland Grainger moved away from the exhibit and continued his round, leaving his friend alone. Moments later, a loud shrill scream pierced the air. Roland ran back to the exhibit and found his friend on the floor – he was a gibbering wreck, and had clearly been terrified by something. In the few minutes it took Grainger to get him outside, his friend told him he had seen a vision of what he believed was an Ancient Egyptian god appear close to him. It held in its outstretched hand a bloody red heart, and beside it stood two humanlike creatures, later described as men with bull's heads, that were staring at him.

Outside, the friend went into shock and was unable to move. He fell silent and his hair turned from dark to completely white. Roland managed to get him home and for several days his friend refused to speak to anyone. Roland felt guiltly that he could not report the incident, as his friend should never have been there.

On a different occasion, a visiting medium declared that the spirit of Nesyamun had spoken to her, revealing that he had been killed by the hands of an enemy in Thebes, and that he would not rest until his killer's descendants had suffered the same fate. Unfortunately, he didn't provide the name of his killer.

Then we have the unrelated story of another female visitor to the museum who was entirely overcome by feelings of absolute desolation as she looked at the Nesyamun display. She claimed to see visions of fire, death and carnage; she described it as ritual slaughter. All around her she saw strange creatures that stared through a curious mist; she believed these were protectors, the underworld guardians of Nesyamun. Without surprise, she apparently declared the coffin and the mummy to be cursed and that she would never again return to the museum.

Perhaps the carnage she envisaged was that caused during German air raids on the city during World War Two. At around 9pm on 14 March 1941, the air-raid sirens began sounding across Leeds as the Luftwaffe aircraft of the German air force returned to bombard the city, dropping bombs during a sustained raid that was more destructive than any other the city endured. In the early hours of 15 March the Park Row museum suffered a direct hit. Countless displays were destroyed, including the unique mummy collection. Three mummies had been on display; two were literally blown to pieces. The third, Nesyamun, survived, but not without some damage. During the initial explosion, Nesyamun had his nose broken off as the lid of his inner coffin was entirely smashed. Nesyamun was removed from the debris, carefully packed and put into storage until he was returned to a display in the relocated museum.

The story surrounding Nesyamun does not end there. In 1989 a more modern scientific examination of the mummy of Nesyamun took place, which hoped to shed light on the cause of his death. One of the original mysteries was what had caused his tongue to protrude from his mouth, and why had the embalmers left it in that state? Perhaps they had been unable to close the mouth as they normally would.

The examination revealed that the tongue appeared to have broken off at some point during the mummification process. The embalmers were required to leave the body in its final state in preparation for the journey to the underworld, so rather than leave it disconnected, they had reconnected the broken part with glue. Despite this revelation, there was still no clue as to how Nesyamun had died.

Eventually, 3,000 years after his death, a forensic examination was carried out, although without any input from the police. The investigating authorities were made up of professionals from the scientific and academic world. Studies had revealed evidence of numerous critical health issues in the body, including arthritis, parasitic worms and a debilitating eye condition. The scientists therefore examined just three possibilities as the cause of his death:

1. A painful tumour.
2. Murder through strangulation.
3. Accidental death caused by a bee sting to his tongue, resulting in him choking to death.

Microscopic examinations of the tongue were carried out. The tongue itself appeared no larger than normal and revealed no evidence of cancerous cells. No cancer was found anywhere in the body, which eliminated the theory that a tumour was the cause of death.

The investigators were also able to dismiss the possibility that Nesyamun was murdered through strangulation, since skin tissue on his neck displayed no marks whatsoever. More importantly, the hyoid bone was still intact. This supports the tongue and is generally crushed when pressure is exerted on it. Thus, although murder was not entirely ruled out, strangulation seems unlikely.

Of the three options, just one remained a distinct possibility. A bee or other type of venomous insect sting could have caused a type of anaphylactic reaction. This would account for the contortion in the face. However, during the course of mummification all bodily fluids were drained from the corpse, so the theory cannot be proved. As with the case of King Tutankhamun, the mystery of the death of Nesyamun remains. Did he die of natural causes, or could it have been murder?

Chapter 15

The Scottish Mummy

The mummy of Ankhesnefer lies in the Kelvingrove Art Gallery and Museum in Glasgow, Scotland, and was originally found by a noted Egyptologist of Greek extraction, called Giovanni D'Athanasi (also referred to as Yanni). His real name was Demetrio Papandriopulo, although he later adopted the pseudonym Giovanni D'Athanasi. His father was a Cairo merchant, having moved there in 1809. In 1813, while still a boy, D'Athanasi entered the service of Colonel Ernest Missett, then British Consul-General, and two years later, in 1815, he entered the service of Henry Salt, who had then moved into that position. From 1817–27, working on behalf of Salt, he was a key excavator at Thebes and became a popular and highly regarded figure among travellers in Egypt during that period. D'Athanasi later became a serious collector of antiquities and his own vast collection was sold in London at Sotheby's on 5 March 1836 and 13–20 March 1837.

It's a popular misconception that the tomb of King Tutankhamun was the first such burial site to be found untouched. D'Athanasi tells us otherwise, and was responsible for recording the first king's burial tomb to be found intact. He recorded the following in his journals:

During the researches made by the Arabs in the year 1827, at Gourna, in the mountain Il-Dra-Abool-Naggia, a small and separate tomb, containing only one chamber, in the centre of which was placed a sarcophagus, hewn out of the same rock, and formed evidently at the same time as the chamber itself... In this sarcophagus was found (the coffin of Nubkheperre Intef), with the body as originally deposited. The moment the Arabs saw that the case was highly ornamented and gilt, they immediately knew that it belonged to a person of rank. They forthwith proceeded to satisfy their curiosity by opening it, when they discovered, placed around the head of the mummy, but over the linen, a diadem, composed of silver and beautiful mosaic work, its centre being formed of gold, representing an asp, the emblem of royalty. Inside the case, alongside the body, were deposited two bows, and six arrows... The Arabs... immediately proceeded to break up the mummy for the treasures it might contain, but all the information I have been able to obtain as to the various objects they found, is, that the Scarab was placed on the breast, without having any other ornament attached to it.

Records indicate that efforts had been made by tomb robbers to tunnel into the tomb from the nearby looted tombs of Shuroy/Iurony, but they had been unable to gain access. Incredibly, the find seems to have been ignored, as the treasures found were distributed (sold) to collectors across Europe, and it was almost a decade later when the facts were recorded by D'Athanasi. The Arabs at Gourna during this period were known for their violence, stemming from battles between the residents of the east and west banks of the Nile, which had long since died out. However, the heritage remained and at Gourna, on several days of the year, violent festivals were held in villages, where all those who owned horses and could ride would convene and participate in races, using long poles to furiously attack one another. So violent were these incidents that eyes were knocked from their sockets and mortal injuries sustained. The fighting Arabs would achieve notoriety once they had murdered a rival during these so-called races, and would be referred to as 'goul' the Arabic word for dragon. This was not a pleasant or friendly region to try to excavate, so D'Athanasi deserves credit for his ability to win over the trust of the local people and use them as part of his excavation team workforce.

In around 1837–39, during later excavations at Thebes, D'Athanasi found the mummy and coffin of Ankhesnefer (meaning: 'May her life be perfect'). He later sold these items to the British Museum. The mummy-shaped coffin is made of wood and painted with hieroglyphic inscriptions. These reveal that Ankhesnefer was the daughter of

Khnomsmes and Isetirdis, and she was responsible for managing her husband's household. Elsewhere on the coffin, colourful scenes relating to the afterlife are painted.

Ankhesnefer is depicted on the coffin lid with a pale yellow smiling face typical for a depiction of a woman during this period. Her eyes are made up with kohl. She is seen wearing an elaborate wig and gilded vulture headdress, and a gilded sun-disc sits on her brow. Inside the casket, the body of Ankhesnefer still lies wrapped in the original linen bandages and shroud that were bound round her some 2,500 years ago.

Various tales surround this mummy, from both its time in the British Museum and in Scotland. One in particular tells how, when the coffin and mummy are viewed by some women, it causes them to weep uncontrollably. One woman explained how she felt a burning sensation on her face and a bright red mark appeared and remained on the right side of her face for several hours after the visit. Another woman believed she could hear the cries of a woman in pain when visiting the exhibit, believing it to come from the coffin. Her husband dismissed her claims and put it down to noise outside the museum. One visitor to Glasgow, Susan Page, was so overwhelmed by a feeling of dread and melancholy during her visit to the exhibit that she wrote to the British Museum and Scottish government, demanding that they return the mummy and coffin to its burial place in Egypt. She felt that the spirit of Ankhesnefer was distressed due to being away from its home land.

Curiously, there exists some mystery surrounding the death of Ankhesnefer. Modern-day X-ray examinations of her remains indicate that she died in middle age and suffered a violent death. There appears to be a large 'sword like' cut to the right side of her skull and face. Egypt in her time was regarded as peaceful, with no wars. This has led to some speculation that the fatal wound may have been inflicted as domestic abuse. Or was she was murdered for a reason which will forever remain a secret?

Chapter 16

The Curse of the Czar's Ring

One of the most curious tales I discovered during my research for this book relates to the late Russian sovereign Alexander III. His widow, in 1898, was going through some of her late husband's desk drawers when she came upon a peculiar looking ring, consisting of a heavy band of gold, in the centre of which was set an extraordinarily beautiful opal, flanked by two diamonds. It was contained in an envelope on which Alexander III had written that the ring had been worn by his father on the little finger of his left hand, and that the original settings were of ancient Egyptian origin.

It is strongly believed that the ring was stolen from the body of a hitherto unidentified Egyptian pharaoh, and that the ring was therefore cursed, bringing tragedy to whoever was in possession of it. When the unfortunate sovereign Alexander II was assassinated by Nihilist bombers in 1881, his entire left hand was shattered, with the exception of the little finger, which remained intact with this ring on it. The rings worn on his third finger were destroyed in the explosion. This ring had been presented to him only a few months previously.

Alexander III took the Egyptian ring from the little finger of his father's torn and mangled hand, placed it in the envelope and hid it in the drawer in which it was found by his widow after his death. The Czarina, not realising that there was any ill luck attached to the ring, took it along with her on her next visit to Copenhagen in the spring of 1898 and left it there in charge of her mother, the queen of Denmark, who died within a year. Finding it among her mother's effects, the widowed empress took it back to Russia and presented it to her son, George, whose sudden death, at the age of twenty-eight, created a sensation. In August 1899 George was found alone by a roadside near

Tiflis in Caucasus. He was discovered by a peasant woman bleeding heavily from the mouth, with his motorcycle laid down beside him. It was not known whether he had suffered an accident or fallen ill and been forced to stop.

The ring was not found among the Grand Duke's belongings, and has disappeared. The tragedies, however, continued. George's title of Heir Presumptive passed to his younger brother Michael. In 1910, Michael named his newborn son George after his late brother. This George also died at a young age; he was killed in a car crash in 1931 at the age of twenty. It has since been suggested by some that the curse of the pharaohs was involved in each of these deaths, and until the ring is found and returned to Egypt, any person who possesses it will be in mortal danger.

Bibliography

Andrews, C., *Egyptian Mummies,* British Museum Press, 1998.

Bauval, R., and Gilbert, A., *Orion Mystery; Unlocking the Secrets of the Pyramids,* Arrow, 1994.

Budge, E.A. Wallis, *The Mummy: A Handbook of Egyptian Funerary Archaeology,* Dover Publications, 1893.

—— *Egyptian Ideas of the Afterlife,* Dover Publications, 1895.

Carter, H., and Mace, A.C., *The Discovery of the Tomb of Tutankhamun,* Dover Publications, 1923.

Clayton, P.A., *Chronicle of* the *Pharaohs,* Thames & Hudson, 1994.

Dane, J., 'The Curse of the Mummy' *Paper Printing History* 17 (2) 18-25, 1995.

Faulkner, R.O., trans., *The Ancient Egyptian Coffin Texts* Vol I-III, Aris & Phillips, 1973.

—— *The Ancient Egyptian Pyramid Texts,* Aris & Phillips, 1985.

—— *The Egyptian Book of the Dead: The Book of Going Forth by Day,* Chronicle Books, 1994.

Lehner, M., *The Complete Pyramids,* Thames & Hudson, 1997.

Murray, M.A., *The Splendour that was Egypt,* Four Square Books, 1962.

Pettigrew, T., *A History of Egyptian Mummies,* North Atlantic Archives, 1834.

Reeves, N., *The Complete Tutankhamun,* Thames & Hudson, 1990.

Reeves, N., and Wilkinson, R.H., *The Complete Valley of the Kings,* Thames & Hudson, 1996.

Shaw, I., and Nicholson, P., *The British Museum Dictionary of Ancient Egypt,* British Museum Press, 1995.

Taylor, J.H, *Unwrapping A Mummy*, British Museum Press, 1995.

Index